TRAILER MECHANICS

TRAILER MECHANICS

A Guide to Making Your
Documentary Fundraising Trailer

by Fernanda Rossi

magafilms

To each and every filmmaker
whose questions and doubts
inspired me to find answers
and ask further questions.

TRAILER MECHANICS
A Guide to Making Your Fundraising Documentary Trailer
by Fernanda Rossi

Published by
magafilms
P. O. Box 717
New York, NY 10028-0044
info@documentarydoctor.com
www.documentarydoctor.com

Cover and interior design by Peter Lukic
Illustration by Zartosht Soltani
Back cover photo by Phoebe Ferguson

ISBN 0-9764581-0-1
Film • Video • Documentary • Fundraising

Printed and Manufactured in the United States of America

PART II • WARM UP THE ENGINE

Section 1 • Understanding Trailer Mechanics

Section 2 • Oiling Your Creative Gears

Section 3 • Catching The Right People In The Headlights

PART III • ON THE ROAD SINGING HAPPILY

Section 1 • Understanding Trailer Mechanics

Section 2 • Oiling Your Creative Gears

Section 3 • Catching The Right People In The Headlights

Every film has credits, and so should a book on filmmaking. *Trailer Mechanics* was made possible by...

Writer	Fernanda Rossi
Project manager	Myra Varadi
Content editors	Maud Kersnowski, Andee Kinzy
Copy editing and proofreading	Maud Kersnowski, Dushan G. Lukic
Book design	Peter Lukic
Cover illustration	Zartosht Soltani
Back cover photo	Phoebe Ferguson
Interviewees	Claire Aguilar, ITVS; Carole Dean, Roy W. Dean Grant; Cheryl Jones, PBS; Michaelle McLean, Hot Docs Festival; Wendy Sax, IFP/NY; Jess Search, Channel 4 TV

Special thanks

Cynthia Carrion
Julio DePietro
Erica Freed
Chris Howard
Tema Levine
Ruth Koeppel
Sonia Malfa
Mitch Micich
Sarah Plant
Richard Schuhmertl
Cara White

And very special thanks to the following for their encouragement

The Borenstein-Burds
Israel and Lillian Burd
Andrea Grynberg
The Kinzy-Schwartzs
The Wagenheims

and my family.

Years ago a written proposal was enough to convey your ideas and beg for dollars, but as technology has advanced, more and more is expected from filmmakers when they ask somebody to help pay for a film. When video became easily accessible, funders began welcoming sample footage. Today, with basic desktop editing systems available on most computers, works-in-progress or trailers are not only welcomed, but demanded. Every funder, investor, and network executive will inevitably ask, "Is there anything we can look at?"

This book will guide you through the process of creating a trailer for those funders, investors and executives to look at. And while much of that process is about story structure and money, it is ultimately also about finding your own voice and being resourceful enough to bring that voice into the world.

You might wonder, how a documentary or its trailer can be structured at all. Aren't documentaries about reality as it happened? Aren't the ideas of "reality" and "story structure" contradictory? Not really. It is true that documentaries document reality, but they also *doc-comment* on reality. And reality unfolds in front of our eyes in a chaotic, unstructured way. It is our minds which select and organize it, so we can process, remember and finally share it with others.

When you make a documentary you systematize the randomness of reality through the scenes you choose, which eventually become the story. You may structure and organize possible scenarios as you film, in the heat of the moment absorbing it all. Or you might choose to do it later like in verité-style documentaries, which capture the complexity of the world in one long take as one would take a deep breath. Then in the quiet of the cutting room starts the slow process of selection and organization. Regardless of when you choose to assert your story, the time to do so will eventually come. Then you will need more than loyalty to reality as it happened to make your story engaging. The exploration of structure means freedom, not confinement. And this freedom comes with knowledge and the capacity to make informed decisions about your story.

Once your story and vision are formulated, the next challenge is bringing that story into the world. Most filmmakers connect this challenge with money, and lots of it. No filmmaker ever said to me, "Gee, I had enough money to do whatever I wanted with that documentary." There never seems to be enough, even if they managed to raise the equivalent of a CEO's salary.

The fact is, not every film with a high budget is a good film. But regardless of how many bad big-budget films we see, we still think that money rules, and to some degree it does. To make good films, particularly documentaries, you need to reclaim the power money took from you. It is not about money but about being resourceful. It is about how you manage to get what you need and how best to use whatever you have. For that reason, in this book, you will not find the latest schemes to become rich overnight, or discuss the latest technology development. What you will find is how to make a documentary fundraising trailer work no matter your budget and gadgets.

Whether you are a first timer or a seasoned filmmaker this book will help you find the principles that will strengthen your criteria and encourage you to become both a critical thinker and savvy artist. Whether you are working with a Super 8 camera or a chip hooked to your eye, your vision and voice should and will remain.

Who this book is for
Beginners, who are looking for guidance on how to get started with their documentary film, will find easy-to-follow steps. Experienced filmmakers will encounter a new perspective to old story challenges and expand their working palette and methodology. In order to accommodate everybody, concepts are explained assuming the only thing we share is the English language and not a film degree.

How this book is structured
Trailer Mechanics is divided into three parts that represent the three stages of every journey: Part I: Tune Up Before You Hit The Road; Part II: Warm Up The Engine, and Part III: On The Road Singing Happily. Each of these parts is divided into three sections, which represent the three elements of every creative endeavor or communication process: 1) the object or message (in this case documentary fundraising trailers) is discussed in Section 1: Understanding Trailer Mechanics. 2) The communicator, (you, the filmmaker) is taken into consideration in Section 2: Oiling Your Creative Gears. 3) The audience or recipient of your message, namely networks, funders, festivals and markets is reviewed in Section 3: Catching The Right People In The Headlights.

Section 1 • Understanding Trailer Mechanics
In this section you will discover how to make your fundraising trailer, from testing your idea to making sure you are really finished with your trailer. You will also find tips on how to maxime your resources.

Section 2 • *Oiling your Creative Gears*

You can know everything about making a trailer, but if you don't understand your process as a filmmaker the whole endeavor can prove fruitless. All the instructions, guides and magic potions in the world are useless if you cannot get up off the couch.

Many people believe that they cannot accomplish their vision because they do not have the right equipment, enough time, loads of cash—fill in the blank with your excuse. Some obstacles are real, but most of them are creative hurdles that need to be overcome. As I say at the beginning of every workshop, "The worst thing that can happen to a film is a filmmaker."

The creative process can be daunting if you are not familiar with it. Most filmmakers are so busy with production that they do not take the time to understand their own process. This section sheds light on these obscure matters. Also included are some warnings about common pitfalls and encouragement to go on in spite of all the complications, of which, believe me, there will be many.

Section 3 • *Catching the Right People in the Headlights*

Trailers, films and art in general do not happen in a vacuum. Someone has to be the recipient, whether that is your family or the entire planet. Since you want to raise money with your trailer, your goal is for a lot of people to watch it. Although I am a big believer in discovering the film you want to make before you find the audience, there is also a healthy level of "audience awareness" needed to raise funds. In order to get you closer to who is out there, what they want, and how they want it, I interviewed a variety of grant-makers, network programming and developing directors, and market and festival organizers that have work-in-progress screenings. Use these interviews as guidelines, not immovable facts. Let them encourage, rather than curtail, your creativity. It is not what these people say, but how you use what they say that will make the difference between a successful trailer and one that sits on a shelf.

How to use this book

Inspiration, unfortunately, does not come with a manual on how to materialize that great idea into something tangible to share with the rest of the world. Hopefully that brief moment of creative bliss will have the power to give you the motivation to look for the necessary tools to make your dream a reality. This book is one of those tools. Rather than using it as a recipe, take it as the starting point, a guide to a process. As with any tool, the more you use it, the more you will find new ways to take advantage of it. I encourage you to explore the pages of *Trailer Mechanics* and reinvent it to suit your specific needs.

This book is structured to resemble the non-linear creative mind. You can get on board at any page and jump around, as you need to. You can read it chapter after chapter, or you can read only Section 1 in Part I, II and III, and then proceed to Section 2. Because I am counting on your creativity, some pages are designed to be torn out so that you can create your own book or books. As you read this book and participate in it you will create your own text with your own experience and knowledge.

Reading vs. Doing

Documentary filmmakers do not scream: Action! at a shoot. But in this case, please do so. Take action with this book. You can only know if the methodologies and suggestions work for you by trying them.

Reading it is a necessary step, of course, but to get the full benefit of this book do not leave it at that. I encourage you to revisit this book regularly. Come back, reread and do the work, whether it is a simple exercise or a week's worth of thinking. Some things will work right away; others will work when you are more confident or may never be right for you. That's OK; only you can tell what is useful to you and your film—after you give it a fair chance. Everything is acceptable as long as it is an action towards the making of your documentary.

PART I
TUNE UP BEFORE YOU HIT THE ROAD

Chapter 1
The Trailer Defined

A fundraising trailer is the first step towards making a documentary. It is a dress rehearsal, a test run, and a great opportunity to learn about your film and yourself. It is also one of the most important elements of your fundraising strategy. It is the best business card you can hand out as an introduction to your documentary. If one image is worth a thousand words, then 24 images per second are worth…well, you do the math.

There are no rules or formal conventions for what a trailer should be or even what it should be called. Anything goes, which can be a good thing at times, but it also can be overwhelming when you need direction. Use the following definitions as guidelines, but remember your creative work is unique and can become the successful exception to the rule.

Trailers and their cousins

A trailer is a five to ten minute piece that represents scenes from your future documentary. It is a visual pitch for your project and used mainly for fundraising purposes.

Throughout your career you probably have heard the terms: trailer, fundraising trailer, work-in-progress, work sample, demo, demo reel, show reel, teaser, featurette, EPK, rip-o-matic, preview, movie trailer and promo. Some people use all these terms interchangeably because they are all short formats with similar purposes, but their differences are meaningful. Understanding these differences will help you to know what people in the business are talking about, but that does not mean you need to have one of each for your documentary.

Demo, Reel, Demo Reel or Show Reel
All of these terms are interchangeable. They refer to a compilation of segments from films that showcase the work of industry professionals. Basically, it is an audiovisual resumé.

The term reel comes from the times of celluloid film. Your reel was literally one reel out of your entire film or a selection of scenes from different films cut together into a single reel that was projected in a screening room.

The term demo, short for "demonstration tape," has been borrowed from the music world. A demo is a song or two from a band delivered to record labels and used to showcase their work in hopes of getting signed. Pretty similar to what filmmakers do, eh? It can also mean a fundraising trailer.

EPK – Electronic Press Kit
Used mainly in the music industry, an EPK is a 3 to 5 minute audiovisual press kit. It has interviews, excerpts of live concerts, and the band's album cover, cut together with the flair of a music video. Websites are quickly outdating this tool.

An EPK can also refer to a CD-ROM publicists send to the press, which contains expanded press kit information, especially photos.

A network may also request an EPK from you, but they are generally referring to clips of your film, to be broadcast during a television interview.

Featurette
A featurette, also known as "the making of" or "behind the scenes," is a 10 to 20 minute promotional tool for a film. It includes actual excerpts of the film as well as footage of the shoot and interviews with the director, cast and other people involved with the film.

These have become popular with the advent of cable television to create a buzz among prospective audiences. Now they are here to stay since DVDs have made them a must in their menus.

This promotional tool is not essential, but it can create more interest. Some viewers like to watch the special features in their DVD's menus. Also, many documentary filmmakers make a living by shooting "behind the scenes" segments on the side.

Preview or Movie Trailer

Been to the movies? The preview, also known as the movie trailer, is a 3- to 6- minute flashy montage of a completed film. The objective is to give enough information to get people interested in buying a ticket. They are a long ad for the film, and like all ads they can be deceiving.

Often documentary filmmakers think a fundraising trailer should follow this format. Not so; grant-makers do not need an ad, but a sample of your storytelling abilities. Luckily the fundraising trailer can easily be re-cut into a preview once your film is done.

Promo and TV spot

A promo, short for "promotional spot", is a 30- second to 4- minute ad or preview of a TV program that the network runs repeatedly. It keeps you informed about programming and their schedules. When such spots publicize an upcoming theatrical screening, it's called a TV spot and it can be 30 to 60 seconds long.

You will not need to make a promo for your documentary. Networks have producers who take care of that, since they have a format to follow which includes lots of graphics with schedule information. You will only have to consider making a TV spot if you are releasing your film theatrically and if there is a budget to run such ads. If you are working with a distributor, they will deliver the spot to the networks and maybe even make a radio version.

It is preferable that you understand what parts of your film have had a good response in test screenings so you can make suggestions to the producer or editor cutting your promo or TV spot in case they ask for your input.

Rip-o-matic

A rip-o-matic is a montage of copyrighted material, film or print that simulates a finished commercial. It belongs in the advertising world. It is their version of a trailer used to sell an idea to a client before they commit the big bucks.

The term is a spin on the word animatic, a storyboard with drawings of the future commercial. When video became accessible, agencies started making their mock commercials with excerpts of real films rented at the local video store, literally "ripping off" from original work—therefore the term Rip-o-matic. Of course, they were not pretending they had shot it themselves; the sole purpose was to sell an idea, mood or look for a commercial.

Teaser

A teaser, as the word implies, is a 2- to 5- minute piece that teases the audience. It is most often edited as a collage of images and sound bites that elicit anticipation and excitement. It doesn't fully expose what the story arc of the documentary will be, but clearly conveys the overall theme.

The teaser was created in the advertising business, as a sneak preview for a full-length commercial. A few images accompany a provocative slogan that keep the viewer wondering what the product is, and a few days later the full spot runs.

These are not recommended for grant applications, as they do not showcase your storytelling skills. They can be useful for a website or for individual investors—people who want to see a little something.

Trailer or Fundraising Trailer

These two terms are used among documentary filmmakers to refer to a short piece that represents parts of their documentary-in-progress, not necessarily in sequential order. Be aware that in the written applications for grants a trailer may also be referred to as a "work sample" or" work-in-progress" or "demo." Always check how such terms are defined within the specific grant application. For the purposes of this book a trailer will always be the same as a fundraising trailer.

Work-in-progress or Rough Cut

A work-in-progress, also called a rough cut, is an incomplete cut of your film that is close to its final sequential order. The length can be anything from 15 minutes to the entire film. The degree of "roughness" and incompletion not only refers to the length, but also to the amount of postproduction you have done on the film. A work-in-progress often will lack its final mix and sound editing, as well as proper titling or licensed footage.

grant-makers that provide finishing funds request works-in-progress rather than trailers. While clearly these funders do not expect a finished film, that does not mean they want to see an unpolished sloppy piece. Deliver the best you can.

Works-in-progress or rough cuts are also used for test screenings, fundraising events and film markets.

Work Sample

A work sample, generally requested by grant-makers, refers to a completed piece from a previous film you directed or produced, cued to the section you want them to watch.

If you are a first-time filmmaker who does not have a body of work, grant-makers will often accept your trailer as a work sample.

Though you will not need to make all of these short pieces for your documentary, you might come across many of these terms. More importantly, they can inspire you to think of new ways to approach the making of your trailer.

Trailers Specifics: Length, Medium, and Content

Now that you have met the family, let's get to know the member of it with whom we will be working, the trailer (or fundraising trailer). Once again, there are no hard and fast rules, just overall guidelines, some of which change with market trends.

Length

Fundraising trailers run from 5 to 10 minutes. If you have never made a trailer before, ten minutes probably sounds like it is nowhere near enough time to convey the depth and importance of your documentary, but once you are sitting in the cutting room you will change your mind. It will become painfully obvious, as you try to glean your best images, that a minute can be endless.

Even if you have an abundance of great images, do not indulge yourself by making a 20-minute piece. For many of the major grants over 200 trailers are submitted. Because of this high volume, screeners often are unable to watch more than the first few minutes. You can find a more thorough discussion about this in Section 2: Catching The Right People In The Headlights, chapters 11 and 12.

Medium

You can shoot the footage for your trailer in video or even film, but your final cut should be delivered on VHS—as per the day of the printing of this book. That is the medium that most networks, grant-makers and potential investors (including your relatives) have in their screening rooms and offices.

In this day and age of DVDs and CD-ROMs, it is tempting to have your trailer presented in these digital formats to give you and your piece the cutting edge. Do not succumb to these technological temptations—they can backfire. Not everybody has a DVD player at home and in the office to screen your disc. And while many computers have this capability, do you really want your trailer screened on a 14-inch monitor? If you are really committed to one of these formats, check the grant application. Most grant-makers specify what format they will be screening on, and that is VHS in most cases.

Content

The content, the images and sound you choose to represent your topic or issue is the backbone of your trailer. As such, how to choose these specific elements and how to structure them is covered in detail throughout the following chapters, but there are a few things to consider before you delve into the rest of the book.

Your trailer is just one piece of a much bigger picture called your fundraising strategy. It will not have the entire responsibility of communicating all aspects of your future film, but it will carry the heaviest load.

Unlike your finished film, your trailer will rarely be shown on its own. If you are having a fundraising event at home, you will be there to introduce it. When submitting the trailer for grants, a proposal will accompany it. But the trailer is your kicker. It proves that you can take all your wonderful ideas and translate them into moving images. For a few minutes you can captivate your audience in a way no proposal or personal presentation can. You have to use that brief magical moment wisely and make it consistent with the rest of your fundraising plan. A good trailer can be the last straw needed to get an investor to sign a check or to make your project a finalist in a grant evaluation.

As I stated earlier, filmmakers often mistake their fundraising trailers for movie previews, those snappy, flashy, music video-style pieces that movie studios produce to sell their films. The purpose of a preview is to convince the viewer to purchase a ticket for the film. For this reason, they do not tell the story of the film, just hint at it. The purpose of a trailer is to raise money. Grant-makers and networks want to learn through your trailer that a) you have a compelling, engaging story, and b) you are capable of telling that story. To show them this you need to present complete scenes that explore your topic in detail and reveal the style and tone in which you will tell the story. The only characteristic of a preview that you want to emulate is leaving your viewer wanting more. Everything else won't work.

When it comes to content, think of your fundraising trailer as a short film without an ending rather than an MTV spot.

Before you determine any of these characteristics, you should always check your grant application or check with your contact at the network for their specifications.

When to Make a Trailer

It is never too early to make your trailer, because it is never too early to begin raising money for a project. The first question prospective funders will ask you is, "Can I see something?"

Even if you do not have any footage you can make a trailer. There are a number of ways to visually represent your future film.

You may end up making several trailers over the life of you film or you may just use the same trailer for the entire length of the production. Some filmmakers even use their trailer as a preview once the documentary is done. Because each film is different, it is difficult to pinpoint why some trailers continue to be representative of a project while others need to be replaced. Often a new trailer is required when the story takes an unexpected narrative turn. Only you know if the trailer reflects the story accurately; that is why you are the best judge of when to start cutting a new trailer. Do not shy away from cutting a new trailer if you need to. Today's technology makes creating or updating your trailer cost-effective enough that you do not have to settle for one that does not represent your film in the strongest way possible. You do not want to submit a grant application with a note reading, "Don't mind this trailer, the film is going to be much better."

Raising Money and Support for your Trailer: Beyond the Grant Application

When most filmmakers start thinking about making a trailer, it is primarily to submit it as part of a grant application. But a trailer can, and should, play a major role in your strategy to raise money for your film. The possibilities for financing your film today are wide and varied.

While your trailer will have a busy life visiting foundations, you should also consider also using it for:

- Networks and cable outlets—some provide developing or finishing funds.
- Festivals and markets—those with pitch sessions or screenings of works-in-progress.
- Private investors or donors
- Corporate investors or donors
- Fundraising parties—in the comfort of your home or at another venue.
- Website—for an online marketing campaign and donations.
- Outreach and special programs—see example below.

Outreach and Special Programs are a major part of many completed films' distribution plan, but you can use a similar format with your trailer to approach interested communities and increase funding. Therefore, I thought it useful to give an example.

Filmmaker and marketing consultant Mitch Teplitsky broke into this territory when he put his trailer to work for him. His documentary-in-progress, *Soy Andina*, narrates the life of a Peruvian woman living in New York who goes back to her town in the high Andes to officiate a traditional fiesta. Mitch reached out to the public at schools, conferences, and other venues to bring the experience portrayed in the film closer to North American audiences. To achieve this, he screened the trailer, had the protagonist perform and teach traditional dances, and encourage a debate on immigration and integration. His wise outreach strategy not only financed part of the completion of his film, but more importantly it developed an audience for the completed film.

So when you think of your trailer, take the highway. Don't forget to include it in your budget, your fundraising strategy and, like a business card, to carry it with you wherever you go. Because you never know!

Chapter 2
So you want to make a trailer for a documentary?

Before you invest time and money into making your trailer, let's make sure you are on the right track to a successful relationship with your documentary. Rewind to the first date with your film and see if it was meant to be.

You and your idea — Testing your commitment

Making a documentary is a long-term relationship. So you need to know if you are truly committed to it. Committed, and passionate enough, to think, talk, write, shoot, and watch footage about this person or topic constantly. This means every waking hour and even some sleeping ones for the next three, four, five, even ten years. Are you ready to live with this film?

If your jaw dropped at the mere thought of this level of dedication, maybe your motives are not clear. Unlike documentarians who work for networks, you will not have a full-time fully paid team of creative and technical professionals or a budget provided by somebody else to fuel your enthusiasm through the rough times. The more scarce your resources, the deeper your commitment must be.

Do not be too quick to drop your project altogether because of lack of money or uncertain intentions. By knowing what motivates you to pursue your documentary you will find the commitment and passion that will take you through the whole process, regardless of resources.

Ask yourself, "Why do I want to make this documentary?"
Your response is probably similar to one of the following:

a. This film if about me. My story must be told.

b. It's such a cool character; it would be really cool to make a film about him/her. And it's going to be a cool film, of course.

c. The world must know that this is happening, or people really need to know about this thing.

d. I can relate to the struggles or characteristics of this person. There is something unique about his/her way of seeing life that speaks to me directly. Or, this thing happening has a lot to do with my values and the overall theme of my life.

a. Personal Documentary

If you answered *a*, then you are making a personal documentary. Personal documentaries are a recent phenomenon, a more common one in the United States than other countries.

A personal documentary is a creative choice about how to approach your topic, but it still does not answer the question as to why you are making this film. You have to take the Olympian leap of detaching yourself from your "self." There is You, the filmmaker and You, the character.

As the filmmaker, you have to have the commitment to follow the character through the entire length of the project. This commitment should be even stronger in documentarians making personal films, since in reality they are working a double shift, one as the stressed filmmaker and the other as the vulnerable character of the film.

Go back to the answers above and ask yourself: What about my own story interests me?

b. Fascination—the cool factor

If your answer was similar to *b*, your interest in this topic or person stems from a sense of fascination. Most likely you had a unique experience or a moment of bliss and wanted to share it. Exotic people, places or events can provoke these feelings.

Living in New York, I bump into "cool" people on a daily basis. There is a temptation for the documentarian around every corner. Your last vacation or a hotdog eating contest can also be the reason for your hypnotized gaze. Maybe making a film about this gives you an excuse to go back over and over to that paradisiacal place or a reason to meet and chat with those funny-crazy-cool people who can eat so many hotdogs. Nonetheless, filmmaking is an expensive and time-consuming excuse to revisit places or people of fascination.

In addition, "cool" is not a convincing argument for grant-makers or investors. Even if you can pass some of your fascination on to them, over time you will be the one needing more than that initial infatuation in order to stick to the project.

Fascination can work on its own, but only if you can find 25 synonyms for the word "cool." That is what you will be doing if this is your primary connection to the topic or character of your film. Your story will be a rediscovery of this fascination over and over. A good example of this sort of filmmaking is 2003 Academy Award nominee *Winged Migrations*, by Jacques Perrin, which lends itself to endless fascination. Each shot is a rediscovery of the beauty of our planet from the privy point of view of our feathered friends and the audience gasps at every shot.

Fascination can also be the starting point, like that sassy guy or girl who looks at you from across the crowded room. Sparks fly. You both walk towards each other in amazing synchronicity... then reality strikes. Is he married? Was she really looking at you or the guy behind you? Or, Yes! You both hit it off. Now you have to work on developing a relationship. Similarly, a topic or character can attract you, and that attraction can propel you into action. You start researching and shooting. You are driven. You are excited. But eventually, as with all relationships, the initial attraction wears off and you will have to rely on deeper motivations to continue your film.

You can test your level of fascination in an inexpensive manner, the way students of the Russian filmmaker Sergei Eisenstein did when celluloid was scarce in the early 20th century with photography and text. Exotic people can make a great collection of portraits that you can display at a wide variety of venues. Or your last vacation can become a great travel essay or magazine article. And that crazy unforgettable weekend at the Mermaid Parade in Coney Island can make a one-of-a-kind hand-made book you can share with your friends over tea.

Choose a medium of expression that is not as expensive and time-consuming as making a documentary. It will give you the chance to experiment with the topic or character free of technical and production hassles. It will also help you test it with an audience. Most importantly, it will give you a sense of closure and accomplishment if there is nothing else to explore. Then you can move on to the next great idea on your list.

If, on the contrary, when you are done you feel a lot remained unsaid and unexplored, then go for a second round with a video camera. That initial attraction might pay off, after all. You could be on your way to a very good trailer that will raise money and in-kind donations.

Of course, there are events that are one-of-a-kind and once-in-a-lifetime. Then by all means, shoot. Shoot a lot. However, just because you shot it does not mean you have to cut a five-part series. Start with a short and see how it goes. You can always add if you feel it merits the investment.

Please check answer *d* because you still need to know the real reasons behind your desire to make this documentary.

c. Moral obligation—the activist's answer

Answers that come closest to *c* are based on a sense of duty. You experience something that needs society's attention: Child labor, teenage pregnancy, the crossed-eyed koala's extinction. The activist in you is called into action and the artist in you cannot be left behind.

Before the filmmaker/activist in you gets too involved, remember that there are over 100 television and cable channels that keep people informed of the miseries of the world. There are also hundreds of non-profit organizations taking care of those people's needs at a fraction of the cost of your film. That said, now that six conglomerates own all the media outlets in the world, your unique perspective on an issue is desperately needed. But if a sense of duty is your only motivation, when you realize that your contribution is not as significant as you thought it would be, you will grow resentful towards the very same topic that once made you compassionate.

My brutal awakening to the pitfalls of moral obligation as motivation came after I had finished my short documentary on tourism for the blind called "On the Edge." It won an award and gained a lot of attention in certain circles. Because of this, I felt the topic could be explored further.

I approached the director of the non-profit organization who had advised me on the making of the short. If we worked together to raise a mere $20,000, I could make a feature-length documentary that could bring social awareness to avoid discrimination of blind people in public places, as well as an endless line of contributors ready to write a check to her organization.

After perusing the budget, she looked up at me without a trace of enthusiasm. "If I could raise $20,000 right now, I could pay more instructors to teach the kids how to read Braille. With $20,000, I could print thousands and thousands of brochures as well as organize workshops and discussion groups that would both increase public awareness and bring contributors. With $20,000 I would most definitely not make a film."

I was dumbfounded; I was also very young, I must add. She cut the tense silence with a polite "I'm sorry" to which I replied with an equally polite "I understand." She certainly had her priorities in place. I was the one who was not clear about mine. She clearly did not need this film as I was naively trying to communicate. I was the one who needed to make it, and I failed to convey the true reasons and personal values that were inspiring me.

Like with the cool documentary, moral obligation can be a good starting point. It is more persuasive than fascination to grant-makers, networks and investors. Ultimately, we all want to be part of changing the world into a better place, but do not let your sense of duty cloud your filmmaking vision. Once again, use moral obligation to discover the personal values that will keep you committed to the project.

If you are still uncertain about your reasons for making this film, and you have been moved to action by an issue that needs attention, then give it your attention in person. Call a non-profit and offer to become a volunteer. Volunteering a few hours a month not only can be rewarding, but it also can give you a sense of closure with the issue. And if the topic is meant to be a film, you will have developed very valuable relationships which will pay off later when you are ready to make the trailer and documentary. The time you spend volunteering will put you in touch with your convictions for making this film, something discussed in answer *d*.

d. The Value of Values—your own documentary

Hopefully, it is obvious by now that all the answers lead you to *d*. You and your values are the only reason why you should be making a film. You and your values are the only reason why you should be embarking on this long, costly adventure. No amount of fascination or moral obligation will carry you through at the eleventh hour to finish the film. But you will be there all along—you and your convictions.

The dictionary definition of value is:

> The value or values of a person or group are the moral principles or beliefs that they think are important in life and that they tend to live their lives by.

Your values are determined by a series of factors such as the society you grew up in, parental beliefs, religion, generational trends, class, etc. These values shape the way you see and interpret your life and all things around you. You might think they describe reality, but they are just a construct by which we choose to live. Examples of values are: If you work hard, you will be rewarded at the end of your life; If you do what you love, money will follow; When we accept who we are, we learn to accept others.

In order to connect to your film in a meaningful way, you need to align your values to its theme. Ask yourself what you strongly believe in. What one sentence describes the way you interpret reality?

These questions will help you find what you care the most about, and from their answers you can get inspired to write down your life value.

Use the following questions as a guide:

a. What are the recurrent themes in your life? (e.g., I always fight against all odds to achieve something. I find creative solutions to things that are not believed possible. I always get something positive even out of terrible experiences.)

b. What are the three things that you value the most in life? (e.g., Relationships, honesty and loyalty. Perseverance, originality and open-mindedness.)

c. How do your friends and relatives describe you? Do they agree with your assessments above?

d. What would you do if you only had 24 hours to live? How about six months or one year?

e. What would you do with a million dollars? What would you do with five million dollars? What if you had to spend it in less than a year?

Keep on quizzing yourself until you have a list that represents you and the things you care about. Then go over your list and highlight those values or themes that will also be represented in your future documentary. Basically, what do you and your documentary have in common?

When your values are clearly related to the theme of the film, you will know exactly why you are making your film. Then finding a way to make it will not seem so daunting and the story will flow naturally.

This is true for all documentaries, including personal documentaries. Aligning your own values to a film about yourself might seem redundant, but you need to be clear about what part of yourself you will be exposing and why. Instead of looking for something in your documentary that resonates within you, look for the part of you and your documentary that resonates with the rest of the world. In essence, what aspect of your personal story is universal?

Being aware of the values you share with your documentary gives you a wealth of information to draw from. Your values hold the answers for story development. They give you strength through production complications. And, in the end, you have the satisfaction that you made a film that speaks with your own voice.

Animator and documentarian Doug Ing is a case in point. He told me he was done with his film. More precisely, he wanted to believe he was done. He had spent six months editing and animating his documentary and did not know how to turn it around.

Doug was under the spell of fascination. His film is about a Chinese man who in 1963 created a calendar with pin-up girls coupled with a joke of the day. Thirty years later he is still figuring out marketing gimmicks to sell the 200,000 calendars he had ordered.

Since Doug lacked a core connection to his film, he ran out of ways to solve structural problems. I could have given him a list of quick fixes, but that would have made it my film, not his. It also would have been a short-term solution. Instead I asked him, "Why do you want to make this film?" He replied, "I like quirky people."

"Quirky" doesn't keep you glued to a monitor for six months animating calendar photos. So I said, "What will happen if you don't finish the film?" He immediately answered, "That's not possible. I will do anything it takes to get this film done."

This is an interesting response from someone whose sole motivation was to portray quirky people. As it turned out, all his previous documentaries were about quirky people who persevered against all odds to achieve their quirky dreams. Doug discovered in our consultation that he shared many values with the characters he filmed. His style might not be as quirky, but it is certainly different—filled with unexpected images. Needless to say he is very persistent and does not give up easily, just like the Chinese man who is still trying to sell his 30-year-old calendar.

We restructured the story based on these new discoveries. Despite the fact that previously he was convinced not much else needed to be done for his film, he was very happy when I suggested some more animation. Actually, he was looking forward to it. He only wished he had known about his connection to his documentary when he started it.

If you are one of those filmmakers who are eager to run with a camera, spending time thinking about what motivates you might seem like a waste of time; but the more you know about yourself and your film the easier it will be to make it.

You, your idea and your documentary—Can it be a film?

Whether you are a novice or experienced filmmaker, you probably think all your ideas are films. But this is not true. Not all your ideas must become films or even have the potential to do so, especially when filmmaking is such a demanding form of expression.

Why, then, are we so convinced that only film can fully materialize our ideas? There are two reasons: one is cultural/technical, and one is creative. The cultural/technical reason is the democratization of the technology necessary to make films. Today, choosing to make a film is not as far-fetched as it was 50 years ago. As the possibility is available, quite logically, many more people opt for it than they used to. But just because it is possible does not mean you have to do it. As an artist you can choose from a variety of mediums. The only reason for choosing film should be the potential of your idea to develop into an audiovisual story and nothing else.

The other reason artists feel compelled to express themselves with film is an unwillingness to deal with the creative process itself. Unlike painting or writing, where it is just you and the blank canvas or paper, with a film there are many things that need to happen before you get involved creatively. To begin with, there are numerous gadgets to purchase and a crew of at least three to hire. Before production has even begun, there is plenty of room for distraction and an opportunity to procrastinate creativity. While busy with these activities you might have the illusion of being engaged creatively. You are working *on* the film, we have to acknowledge that, but you are not working *in* the film. That feeling of productivity is in fact a creative block in disguise. In the end, you are delaying your chance to create. Sometimes choosing filmmaking as a form of expression means choosing not to express yourself.

Once you have determined that the reason you are making this film is not because of technological availability or an attempt to avoid creative involvement, you are ready to test your idea for story and audiovisual potential.

There are two main things to consider:

a. Your idea's ability to evolve as a story.
b. Your story's ability to be represented with images and sound.

a. Story development

To test whether your idea can develop into a story, try this simple experiment. Tell your idea to someone.

For example, tell your spouse about that homeless person outside the ATM who curses at everybody who does not give him any change. Does your spouse look at you blankly and say in a monotone, "That's interesting, honey," and then proceed to tell you that the kids need to be tucked into bed?

Maybe your pitch needs work or maybe your spouse is not your target audience. So try it with a number of people. If they all look at you blankly and say "Interesting," followed by a heavy silence, then your idea might not have the elements necessary to develop into a story.

But let's say you tell the same people that you met a homeless person who recites Shakespeare. Do they want to know more? Are they asking: Which play? How come he knows Shakespeare? Where can I see this person? Why did he end up homeless? Now that is story potential!

When people respond to your idea with questions, they are telling you that you are onto something. Quickly, write down their questioning because these people are volunteering story development strategies.

For testing purposes, that is all you need to know for now. There is more to story development, which will be the main topic of Part II.

b. Images and Sound

To find out if your story can be represented in an audiovisual form, you have to try a new set of experiments.

First observe yourself while you are relating your story. Are you using descriptive images or only abstract concepts? If you are using abstract language, can the concepts become images and sounds?

Try telling your story with imaginary photos. How many photos do you need? One, five, twenty? The more the better. This means your story cannot be encapsulated into one image only.

Next check for sound possibilities. What sounds best describe your story? Do you hear a narrator speaking? Are your characters good communicators? Is this audio complementing the images you came up with? Or can your story only be told and not shown?

Evaluate your answers, and decide whether your story has the potential to become a compelling film that uses images and sound creatively.

Using these experiments, you can conclude whether your idea should become a documentary or not. If you can truthfully answer yes, you will be certain that only making a film will do justice to your story.

Now is a good time to explore to what length you will develop your story. When filmmakers are asked at this early stage what plans they have for their documentary, most of them answer, "It will be a feature-length film with an international theatrical release." Even with the most obscure topics, the answer remains the same. You are in love and committed. Your enthusiasm translates into an aspiration for the biggest, longest and most impressive film ever made.

Ego might also play a role in the pronouncement that your film will be a huge, theatrical feature. The status that comes with the longest, biggest documentary is sometimes a way to compensate for a lack of understanding of story development and market needs.

Use this enthusiasm to begin the process. As reality hits and time goes by, this first vision of grandiosity changes into something more suitable for the story you want to tell. Do not be intimidated by your own big dreams. Keep an open mind and adapt as your film evolves and requires a new format or length.

By this point you are aware of your motivations to pursue a certain idea. You also know that you are fully committed to telling this story that can be represented with images and sound. This is a lot to think about. But with this solid foundation and having dabbled in the basic requirements of a trailer, you are ready to learn how to structure your fundraising documentary trailer.

Chapter 3

Need to swerve creative potholes to get started?

Being a filmmaker means being many different people at the same time. There is the businessperson, the technology expert, the manager, the networker; there is also the story-teller, an artist—the creator of meaning.

Many documentary filmmakers are not comfortable with the term "artist," but in the broadest sense an artist is a creator. Someone who pulls meaning from a collection of scenes, whether fictional or real, is creating something, much as cooks or carpenters do. And while not all cooks, carpenters or filmmakers perfect their works to the level of masterpieces, all of them are creating; therefore they are artists.

This ambivalence towards the word "artist" may explain why there is a shortage of film-oriented information, such as literature, workshops and college curricula designed to help these creators understand the creative process and themselves as artists. The few books that do address these concerns are more likely to be found in the self-help or psychology section of your local bookstore than the filmmaking aisle. Apparently, as long as a filmmaker know how to press the REC button everything will be fine.

Consultations with beginner and senior filmmakers, not the self-help section, led me to realize that expertise and craft has nothing to do with being accomplished and productive. Great stories and films remain undone, not because of inexperience with the technical aspects of filmmaking, but because of inexperience with the creative process and a lack of self-awareness.

To my dismay, even seasoned filmmakers knew very little about their creative process. They knew why they made films or what they wanted to say, but they knew nothing about how their creative patterns worked on a day-to-day basis. Though accomplished, they still had a high level of anguish and heartache, which eventually was forgotten when the lights came up and the applause resounded in the room, very much like a mother after giving birth. Labor pain? What labor pain?

When someone who creates does not understand the process, specific, negative behavior patterns often emerge. A short list includes tantrums, verbal abuse of colleagues, procrastination of different degrees, depression, addiction, snobbish, arrogant behavior, self-neglect and self-deprecation. Over the centuries these symptoms have been mistaken for the normal and natural traits of every artist or creator.

Too often when someone throws a fit, their colleagues lower their eyes and whisper, "He's difficult, but he is sooo talented" or, "She has a drinking problem, but hey, her work is amazing." What these colleagues fail to realize is these people are creating in spite of their issues, not because of them. With the tolerance and silent approval of these symptoms we are all enabling the stereotype to be perpetuated.

But fear not, you can be a good person, have a good life and still create good work. Yes, the creative process is anxiety-driven, but not only is the tortured, suffering artist passé, it can also be avoided.

The question of talent

The question of talent is out of the question, due to the fact that talent and its *measurement* or *appreciation* is a very subjective matter. Every creator has a natural desire to be told that they are talented and a fear of being told that they are not. Acting on these fears and desires is a trap that will neither aid the success nor completion of your project. I assume all filmmakers are talented and that they can all use help to *improve* and finish their films. It is about the work to be done, not the evaluation of talent. Of course, at some point it is necessary to solicit input about your work (to learn more about when and how to do this see Chapter 15). What is not necessary is to ask anybody about YOU or your talent in any way.

At some point almost every filmmaker I have worked with has leaned across the table and in a low voice asked, "Honestly, do you think we have *something* here?" And I answer, "Honestly, does it matter what I think?"

Their ambiguous question hides another direct question—"Am I talented? Am I up to the task? Am I coming up with a good film?" But who is to say you are talented? Critics? History? Your mother? You? They are all biased, you more than all of the others combined.

What if your worst fears came true and somebody told you that you were not talented? What real difference would it make? Sure you might be sad, disappointed, maybe even depressed, but wouldn't you keep working, sooner or later? Let's suppose you believe this person, and that you are indeed the least talented person ever born. Will that be true tomorrow? In ten years? You might perfect your skills to such a degree that your critic will recant and proclaim you talented after all. Or perhaps future generations will consider your lack of talent sheer genius.

Or what if your best-case scenario happened and people you admired and respected told you you were the most talented filmmaker ever? I have seen artists validated with awards and critical acclaim become paralyzed. They either stop producing work for fear of not achieving the same results or they make the same film over and over with different names. They might claim they have discovered their style or voice, but deep inside they know that they are not challenging themselves, that they are stuck.

The question of talent will haunt you, but your job as a filmmaker is not to seek out answers. Your job is to continue working. I used to have a sign on my desk that read, "Am I talented? Nobody knows. Nobody cares. Now get back to work." These days when the talent question assaults me, I call one of my closest friends and say, "I sent you an email with a draft of a synopsis, can you pretend you read it and tell me how good I am." They comply happily since I usually do the same for them. The talent question is a beast to be subdued, not fed. Put the issue aside—forever.

Know yourself

In order to better utilize your unquestionable talent you need to know what type of filmmaker you are going to be or already are. We already have explored the types of films you want to make and why. Now it is time to explore who is the person behind the camera.

To begin with, everybody is a first-time filmmaker, whether you are picking up a camera for the first time or a seasoned pro. At the same time every filmmaker is an experienced human being.

The goal is to have what Buddhist master Shunryn Suzuki calls a beginner's mind, so you can approach every situation with the curiosity and humility of someone who has never been there before. Even if it is your tenth film, this is the first film on this topic, with these characters, in these particular circumstances. In the words of Greek philosopher Heraclitus, "You cannot step in the same river twice, for fresh waters are ever flowing in upon you."

But while you are a beginner, you also have accumulated a vast amount of experience throughout your life, which you can now draw on. Filmmaking is to some extent the combination of a variety of skills used in other art forms and jobs. You can use this previous knowledge to ease your transition into filmmaking. In one way or another, you have done some aspect of filmmaking before.

For example, most journalists have a passion for research and facts. That is a definite plus for documentary filmmakers, but the structure of their films often suffers because they include *all* facts, no matter how insignificant. They fail to realize that while informing the audience is an important part of documentaries, conveying the characters' emotions is equally crucial.

Meanwhile, English majors tend to rely heavily on narration and prefer to cut interviews first, while neglecting the value and power of stand-alone images. Filmmakers with photography backgrounds suffer from the opposite malady. They can tell a story in images, but sometimes they have a harder time accepting that general audiences cannot look at an image for as long as they themselves can.

Finally, those filmmakers that have a background in management or business are great producers. They can multitask, but they cannot sit quietly in the cutting room for more than ten minutes. Their complaint to me is, "I feel I'm not doing anything." I'm sure their editors disagree.

Take a look at the questions below to help you determine which parts of being a filmmaker comes easily to you and which parts you have to work on. Awareness of your strengths and weaknesses will make your process more efficient. There are no right or wrong answers, so be honest.

Inventory of skills
   a. What was your education geared towards (the written word, visual arts, business management, or something else)?
   b. How about your hobbies? Are they oriented towards writing, imagery or interactive?

Whatever your answers to these questions, consider finding assistance in the areas that you do not feel knowledgeable about. If you have strong verbal skills, work with someone who is good with images.
If you are better at telling a story with images, make sure your editor is good with the organization of sound bites and narration.

c. Do you feel comfortable multitasking?

d. Can you handle unpredictability and chaos with minimum stress? Documentary filmmaking is innately chaotic and unpredictable.
If you are more productive in a well-ordered environment, spend extra time planning your shooting and if possible have a production assistant who is more experienced than you are.

e. Can you keep focus for long periods of time?

f. Are you detail-oriented?
If no, the editing process can be gruesome. You might want to consider editors who can work on their own, so you can keep yourself busy with other tasks. The editor will be grateful.

These questions are just the beginning of what hopefully will become a life long learning experience of who you are as a filmmaker. Your film now has a better chance of getting started on the right foot. Being aware of your strengths and weaknesses will enable you to be a more productive filmmaker.

Getting started

If you know yourself at least a little bit, understanding the creative process will be less challenging. At the root of every creative process is fear. You might think of yourself a very self-assured person. But unless you jump out of bed every morning full of energy, go directly to your work space and get going all day long until at the end of the day you feel an amazing sense of satisfaction, and can do so for months at a time, then fear is at work.

As explained earlier, fear or overall anxiety about your work can come out as abusive behavior, arrogance, or even addiction. It also manifests itself as procrastination. Fear comes in so many shapes that sometimes it takes some experience to unmask it. Procrastination is a chameleon and at times looks like real work. Have you ever found yourself neatly organizing your tapes over and over while never actually watching them?

29

By understanding fear and its manifestations such as procrastination, you will be able to streamline your filmmaking, saving time and money along the way.

Fear of losing your mind

Many filmmakers have shared this thought, quietly or as a shout for help. They feel overwhelmed, distracted, tired, unmotivated. Filmmaking requires high energy, a strong drive and multitasking. It is the opposite of writers who sit in front of a blank piece of paper all alone. Both situations, however, create high levels of anxiety.

Sometimes the fear of losing your mind reveals a deeper fear, the fear of discovering through your work a part of you that was safely concealed before you decided to make this film. How will the new information about yourself affect you? Will you have to take action? It can be paralyzing.

Avoid further procrastination and stop all complaining and anguish and become pro-active. Lose and loosen your mind. Let anxiety take over for a moment so you can look at your fears directly. Then take action. If routine feels safe, develop one. If you still lose your mind it will be in an organized productive way. Become familiar with time management techniques. Exercise control in the areas that can be controlled and accept that filmmaking is like life, full of surprises, obstacles and dull moments.

Fear of the unknown

If you are a novice at filmmaking, the fear of the unknown is justified and generalized. As a professional, the fear of the unknown comes associated with the particular project you are starting. It also takes the form of fear of not knowing what to do, fear of appearing unprofessional in front of peers and fear of making mistakes.

If this is the fear that assaults you, you will find yourself, among other things, taking many courses and workshops, reading every textbook, researching beyond what is necessary for your film, hiring people before you have need of them and then blaming them for not performing as expected, buying equipment without a production plan, etc. All these activities are, of course, very necessary and productive, but when these actions are obsessive and rooted in fear they hinder your progress. They become increasingly about quantity and not quality. What is important is balance.

Fear of failure or success

This fear appears as fear of not being good enough, fear of making mistakes, fear of judgment and rejection, fear of not being able to ever finish. If you fear success—nothing more than fear of failure but reversed—you probably have made a negative association with success at some point in your life. You think success will lead to isolation, envy or set you up for higher demands in the future, which you do not feel capable of fulfilling.

Some filmmakers with this form of fear are fueled by the desire to succeed, which only increases their fear of failure. They do not seem to procrastinate and get started right away but as they move forward they dread more and more the approaching finish line and find ways to sabotage the completion of the project.

Other filmmakers are taken over by these fears, sometimes in combination with the ones described above. You will find yourself getting distracted with other tasks or coming up with so many ideas that you are unable to choose any one of them. You may get completely paralyzed sometimes with the excuse that you are "waiting for funding." If you do manage to get yourself started, then you work half-heartedly, miss deadlines and/or lose or misplace important materials.

You might also attempt to hire others too early and immediately complain that they are unable to capture your ideas exactly they way you envision them, so you hire and fire as if you were running a headhunting company. "Nobody understands me" becomes your mantra and it is true. Nobody understands why you want to do your project and do not want to do it at the same time.

Because fear of failure is the most pervasive fear, the entire next chapter is devoted to strategies that can minimize those fears' effect.

Check yourself often to detect procrastination and spare no effort in finding the fear that is triggering it. You can then take proper action.

Writing self-inventories of who you are, what your skills are, what type of film-maker you want to be or what might deter you from filmmaking might seem redundant or feel awkward. Not giving yourself time to ponder these questions is taking yourself out of the equation, leaving your film at the mercy of outside forces. So sharpen your pencil and be present for your documentary from day one.

Chapter 4
Need a pat on the back to get started?

When you shoot an arrow, your eye, the tip of the arrow and the target align. Your eye, your trailer and where you see your film playing also need to be aligned. You will need to imagine the future of your film in full detail. By doing so, you will increase the chances of materializing that future because you will go for it wholeheartedly rather than look down at your feet at every step and bump into lamp posts.

Success. What success?

Imagine you are not here starting the trailer of a film but that you are far down the road with a finished documentary in your hands. Where do you see your documentary playing? Who is coming to the premiere? Who is introducing you? What do you say to introduce your film? In short, you made it! What is your idea of success? How does it feel?

Success means different things to different people. Even in the corporate world where the definition of success seems clear-cut there are many different options. Success may be a six-figure check and a corner office. Or maybe it is starting your own company. Or maybe it is taking early retirement to sail around the world. Filmmakers have possibly an even more diverse menu of definitions to choose from.

Some filmmakers measure their success by whether they sell their films and for how much. Others measure success by the number of festival awards they win. And others still prefer to count full houses or standing ovations or duration of clapping. You can be happy with any one of these or miserable when you attain all but one.

I have been amazed time and again when I hear colleagues express their disappointment at having had "such and such" award but not made "such and such" sale. And days later someone else emails me, "Got the big check, but no awards." That is when I decided happiness has to be included and budgeted into the production plan to avoid stalling in the present and frustration in the future.

Of course, some amount of dissatisfaction is healthy and necessary to help keep you striving for excellence. But permanent disappointment can be paralyzing. You need to figure out in advance what success means to you and do not change your mind once you get it. To avoid that, the next exercise will be your commitment and written record of what success means to you, so when in the future you achieve it you can simply enjoy it.

Exercise 1 – Define Success

Write a few sentences outlining what success is to you. It is a good idea to post this in a prominent place.

If you are not keen on writing, you can express the same thoughts with images. You can make a collage or create the poster of your film and hang it in your workspace.

If you are more of the kinetic type, maybe you want to give your award acceptance speech in front of the mirror or record yourself addressing an imaginary audience.

Choose a technique that matches your skills and have fun. Nobody is watching. *(See Worksheet 1 on page 39)*

Been there, done worse than that

If the idea of being successful feels completely foreign, you can still get started with enthusiasm. Rather than focusing on a bright future, dig into your past for confidence, building material.

At the moment you are probably associating this moment of getting started with other similar moments, which were not as successful. But that can be changed. Some time ago, you might have had everybody telling you your plan or wish was impossible. And still you succeeded. Recall that time in detail. Who said no? What convinced you to go ahead? What strategy did you apply? Even if it was your grand-mother discouraging you from selling lemonade on the steps in the middle of the winter, and you did anyway, letting them freeze and selling them as colored ice... well, that counts. At least once, you succeeded, and you can make it happen again.

Exercise 2 - A positive association

Recall in full detail and write down a breakthrough moment when against all odds, the impossible became a reality thanks to your perseverance or ingenious abilities. List your skills and relive the moment.

You can also tell it to a friend or look for a picture that reminds you of that moment. *(See Worksheet 2 on page 41)*

Living through it

If the future is a mirage and the past is fuzzy, then you might have to convince yourself to get started by embarking on a real-life experience. Instead of working on the real project to which you have certain level of attachment and which will take much longer, do a simpler, shorter documentary, as simple and as short as a one-minute documentary in one day. This documentary is your test run or drill. Something that can put you through the entire process and dissolve all those fears of unknown procedures and disastrous outcomes.

Actors know about these drills to condition the mind. They are called dress rehearsals. I have applied the technique myself for speaking engagements. I go to the room where I will be speaking and walk the perimeter of the space. I sit in different spots. Then I speak to the invisible audience. In my mind I already gave the talk. When it happens for real it is a breeze.

Exercise 3 - The one-minute, one-day documentary

If you have a consumer camera and desktop editing system—even the simple one that comes with most computers today—you can do this exercise. If you do not have access to this equipment yet, you can borrow it for a day, team up with someone or you can do it with still photos.

Early morning
Choose a topic. If you have a lot of ideas draw one from a hat. It can be anything, your husband's smoking habit or the cat's ability to disentangle wool, anything. This is about getting it done, not about getting it perfect.

By 10am

Start pre-production. Choose locations, characters, gather your equipment, etc.

By 1pm

Start shooting. Do not shoot more than half an hour total. View your material. Select, digitize or if you are working with a still camera, develop the photos or download the digital files to your computer.

By 4pm

Start editing. Do you need voice-over? How about the credits? Music?

At 9pm

You can have a screening in you living room with your cat. Congratulations! You are a filmmaker.

Do this exercise with your mind focusing on getting the job done, not on quality. Take it also as a chance to see how you handle stress and unpredictability.

Love your neighbor who loves your work

Before you embark on this film journey, you will also want to select some very important travel mates. No matter how well you know your creative patterns and rely on your own internal voice, there will be those moments that require outside emotional support. Before you find yourself sharing the perils of your project with strangers on the bus or at the bakery, list those friends and relatives you can count on for the occasional late-night call.

Make sure they are not part of the crew. Some filmmakers recruit their producers, for this task of patient listening, unconditional support and cheerleading. Sooner or later the professional relationship suffers and the film suffers, too.

Also avoid fellow filmmakers as potential supporters. Save those relationships and their valuable time for the critical questions about filmmaking. If they are in between projects, they can spare some time. But bear in mind filmmaking is their passion; it could happen that instead of listening and supporting you unobtrusively, they might be more eager to give advice. They will tell you what to do according to their experience, goals and formulas of success, all of which may or may not be the same as yours. In the end, you might have a hard time distinguishing your voice from theirs. By all means, become part of the filmmaking community, but do not have unreasonable expectations from your peers. The fact that they can make their own films does not mean they can help you with yours.

Choose your allies carefully from among all the people you know, not just the ones you think are creative or understand the film business. Do not enlist more than three. Pick people who have known you from the time you were a normal sane person, so they are not shocked to see you cry inconsolably because you intended to submit the synopsis in Helvetica and you did in Geneva after staying up all night. They will know that you are just going through a stage.

List these peoples' special skills and qualities. Who in your immediate circle of friends and relatives are good listeners? Who have natural enthusiasm for life and sees the bright side of everything? Who are satisfied with his or her life and feels happy about your successes? Who are curious and always ask questions about your ideas instead of forecasting gloom and doom? Who are generous and compassionate? These are your unconditional allies.

Exercise 4 – Board of Unconditional Allies.
Write down as many people who might qualify as you can think of. Now imagine you are talking to these people. How do you feel after speaking to them? Have you gone through similar situations in the past? How did it turn out? What is going on in this person's life? Are they settled or is their life in upheaval? Have they been supportive of your past endeavors? Edit your list until you have the finalists with back-up names for safety. Keep your chart handy. In moments of stress you will need it. *(See Worksheet 4 on page 43)*

Hopefully all these pats on your back will push you forward. The first step is often the hardest but it is also the most meaningful. It will set you in the right direction and tell you something about you: You can do it. Do it right now.

Worksheet for Exercise 1

My Definition of Success

I will feel successful when…

_____

_____

_____

_____

_____

_____

_____

_____

If that fails, I will still feel successful if at least me and the documentary…

_____

_____

_____

_____

_____

_____

_____

_____

(Cut along line)

Worksheet for Exercise 2

Positive Associations

Once, I thought I couldn't…

_____

_____

_____

_____

_____

_____

_____

_____

But I still managed to…

_____

_____

_____

_____

_____

_____

_____

_____

41

Worksheet for Exercise 4

Board of Unconditional Allies

	Name	Strongest asset
1.		
2.		
3.		
4.		
5		
6.		

These interviews are for you to get familiar with how people in the industry operate. This information is not conclusive, nor exhaustive. When it is time for you to send out your fundraising trailer or work-in-progress, go to their website and look for the most up-to-date information regarding their guidelines for submission.

Chapter 5

Who are they in the network world?

Let me introduce you to two of the many, many networks that fill the planet's airwaves.

Channel 4 TV – London, UK.
Jess Search
Editor, Independent Film and Video
General Website: www.channel4.com
Producers' information website: www.4producers.co.uk

Channel 4 was started in 1982 and is one of the 5 free air channels in the United Kingdom. It transmits across the country, except for some parts of Wales. More than three-quarters of the United Kingdom's population watch Channel 4 services in the course of an average week.

This network is a publicly owned corporation whose board is appointed by the television regulator, the Independent Television Commission / OFCOM (after December 2003), in agreement with the Secretary of State for Culture Media and Sport. Unlike the BBC, Channel 4 receives no public funding. It is funded entirely by its own commercial activities. It is a publisher/broadcaster. It does not produce its own programs but commissions them. There are 40 to 50 commissioners across the whole channel, currently 6 in documentaries.

Note: Feel free to cut out and bind this section.

Public Broadcast Television – Virginia, U.S.A.
Cheryl Jones
Senior Director of Program Development & Independent Film
www.pbs.org/producers

Founded in 1969, PBS is a private, non-profit media enterprise owned and operated by the nation's 349 public television stations with headquarters in Alexandria, Virginia. Serving over 90 million people each week in all 50 states, Puerto Rico, the U.S. Virgin Islands, Guam and American Samoa, PBS offers quality programs and education services on noncommercial television, the Internet and other media.

PBS oversees program acquisition, distribution and promotion; education services; new media ventures; fundraising support; engineering and technology development, and video marketing. There are six executives on the Senior Programming Team, led by President and CEO Pat Mitchell, a former independent producer herself. Then there are three genre directors who have special expertise with certain types of programs.

Chapter 6

What do they have to say about fundraising trailers and works in progress?

1. How many documentary submissions do you receive per year and how many do you select or finance?

Jess Search, Channel 4: Personally, tons! I don't count them all as they come by email, by phone, at meetings, as well as on paper. My department, Independent Film and Video, spends about £3 million a year on about 35 hours of commissions and another 20 hours of acquisitions of completed documentaries such as *Born Rich, Capturing the Friedmans*, etc.

Cheryl Jones, PBS: PBS receives thirty-three hundred submissions per year. For just independently produced programs, during Fiscal Year 2001—the most recent year for which we have complete records—there were 290 separate incoming Program Acceptance Agreements (PAAs) with some independent producer involvement. Some of those represented entire seasons of series and others individual episodes of series like P.O.V., American Experience, Frontline, The Independent Lens and Great Performances.

2. Do you select American issue documentaries or also international?

JS, Channel 4: Well, we are UK, but we do take more US stories than any other foreign countries.

CJ, PBS: We select and become involved with both domestic and international documentaries and programs in the areas of science, history, natural history, drama, performing arts, culture, public affairs, and news.

3. Do you select or finance co-productions with foreign countries?

JS, Channel 4: Yes, not very many though as it's often hard finding co-production partners with the same editorial needs and the same tone as Channel 4. It's easier with science and history than with social or narrative documentaries.

CJ, PBS: Yes.

4. What type of documentaries is your organization interested in: historical, social issues, personal journey, biographies, mockumentary?

JS, CHANNEL 4: Channel 4 is interested in all kinds.

CJ, PBS: We want documentaries that are engaging at the same time they are informative and responsible towards the topic discussed or the character portrayed. We favor geographic and ethnic diversity as well as a fresh perspective. We hold the highest number of slots for documentaries among all networks and cable in the United States.

PBS is committed to giving viewers a well rounded, entertaining, and enlightening multi-media experience. We remain dedicated to our mission of providing a public service to our viewers and working with our member stations to offer a unique voice in their communities, one committed to the needs of our audience and their families regardless of commercial concerns or pressures. To that end, we believe that our programming should seek to enrich the communities we serve by highlighting diverse cultures, opinions, and stories. Program topics should be interesting to a wide audience and be of a high caliber throughout all elements of the production, with a well-crafted storyline, strong visuals, and a clear purpose.

We continue to seek programming drawn from the broad areas of News and Public Affairs; Science and History; Drama and Performing Arts, and Children's Programming. Programs and proposals offered to PBS for consideration should enhance and/or complement the current schedule of programs.

Below are a few examples from the PBS program library of what we are looking for:

Observational Documentaries: Frontier House

Commanding Heights: The Battle for the World Economy

Biographies: American Experience "Jimmy Carter"

American Masters "Sidney Poitier: One Bright Light"

American Drama: American Mystery! Special "Skinwalkers"

PBS Hollywood Presents "The Gin Game"

Science and history: NOVA

American Experience "The Murder of Emmett Till"

Arts & Culture: Great Performances

Children's Programming: Sesame Street, Clifford

News & Public Affairs: Frontline, NOW with Bill Moyers

Independent Film: P.O.V., Independent Lens

5. Are there any styles you would be more interested in selecting or financing? E.g.: Verite, experimental, investigative report/expose, etc.?

JS, CHANNEL 4: My department specializes in experimental, controversial and new talent films. You can see more info about this at our website, www.4producers.co.uk.

CJ, PBS: None more than the other. Depends on the program.

6. How important is the previous work of the filmmaker/producer?

JS, Channel 4: Very important for some budgets and slots and not just the filmmaker's track record, the production company and exec producer is also crucial. That said, we have specific opportunities for new filmmakers, more than any other British broadcaster by far, and obviously for those we take risks without studying track records.

CJ, PBS: It's very important if we are looking at a proposal or work-in-progress that the filmmaker has a track record. If it's a complete work, not as important.

7. What do you consider a good filmmaker/producer's track record? E.g. major festival awards, theatrical release, significant outreach.

JS, Channel 4: It depends entirely on the job being discussed.

CJ, PBS: It's the quality and content of the work that we are interested in. Outreach and web sites are important components that add value to a project.

8. How important is it to have financing in place for you to consider the project?

JS, Channel 4: Not important. Whether we want the idea or not is everything.

CJ, PBS: Producers are encouraged to raise the majority of financing for their programs from sources other than PBS. Financing in place, or at least partial financing, is always helpful.

9. What is the submission process? E.g. tape only, tape with press kit, pre-formatted proposal and tape but no other materials, etc.

JS, Channel 4: It depends on whether it's for completed documentaries or new ideas.

CJ, PBS: Complete guidelines for submission can be accessed at www.pbs.org/producers. All submissions must be accompanied by a signed proposal release form, available at pbs.org/producers or by calling 703.739.5289. The process varies slightly for a complete work, work-in-progress or web proposal.

10. What is the selection criteria and process? E.g. two rounds of panelists, unanimous vote, etc.

JS, Channel 4: No formal process, the commissioning editor will consider it and then give a unilateral response.

CJ, PBS: Programs and proposals are approved for broadcast and/or funding during two commissioning rounds per year—April and October. The Senior Programming Team convenes monthly to discuss recommended titles, identify any outstanding questions and/or materials, and determine those projects that should move forward to the commissioning round. At the commissioning round, all final green-lighting decisions are made. Producers are notified shortly thereafter.

11. How long does it take a filmmaker to receive an answer?

JS, Channel 4: Usually you get a no to an idea within 4 weeks. A yes can take longer. Tapes take much longer to be considered, depending on the back-log!

CJ, PBS: Because the number of proposals we receive varies greatly, we do not have a standard time-frame in place for a response. We are committed, however, to getting producers answers on their proposed projects as quickly as possible, usually within 4-6 weeks.

12. What is the filmmakers obligation to your organization after they have been selected? Do you have input or final say during the making/editing? Share revenues of the film?

JS, Channel 4: YES! We have editorial control effectively of the final film and need to have so legally. Filmmakers share revenues.

CJ, PBS: The filmmaker has editorial control over their project. All other conversations regarding the working relationship and financial model are negotiable.

13. Would you consider selecting/funding or financing a pitch or proposal without watching a trailer or work-in-progress?

JS, Channel 4: Yes.

CJ, PBS: Depending on the producer involved and the track record of that person, potentially yes.

14. How long should a trailer or work-in-progress be?

JS, Channel 4: 5 minutes.

CJ, PBS: We will look at works-in-progress of any length.

15. Do you watch trailers in their entirety?

JS, Channel 4: If they are 5 minutes, yes.

CJ, PBS: We would watch the entire work-in-progress.

16. In how many minutes should a trailer or work-in-progress "hook" you?

JS, Channel 4: Straight away.

CJ, PBS: The sooner we identify a compelling storyline and characters the better. It's ideal if it builds up within the first 2 to 3 minutes.

17. Are the first two to three minutes of a trailer or work-in-progress really critical in your decision process or do you evaluate the whole regardless of how the trailer is structured?

JS, Channel 4: Yes, the first few minutes are critical.

CJ, PBS: The first few minutes are critical because that's when you've got the opportunity to get the audience interested. We look at a good bit of a work-in-progress. If we get particularly interested in it, we'll watch the whole tape. We can tell we are not interested in the 20 minute range, though it's not always sequentially viewed.

18. Do you think a trailer (5-12 minutes) is a fair way to judge a full-length documentary? Why?

JS, Channel 4: I'd only watch the trailer if I was looking for proof of something specific, such as "Can this character sustain a film?" That can be judged very quickly.

CJ, PBS: We need to see the completed work before making the final decision to broadcast a program.

19. In your opinion is a fundraising trailer more similar to a music video, a movie preview, a commercial spot or an excerpt of a film?

JS, Channel 4: An excerpt of the film.

CJ, PBS: We prefer works-in-progress, and that's an excerpt of the film.

20. What should a trailer or work-in-progress tell you about the filmmaker and/or topic?

JS, Channel 4: It depends on what the project is.

CJ, PBS: It should tell us the quality of the production elements. If there is a compelling storyline, it's well researched and documented and if the producer is capable of bringing it to conclusion.

21. How important is it in a trailer or work-in-progress to convey:

> a. storytelling abilities?
> b. filmmaker's unique voice or style?
> c. access to the characters/interviewees?
> d. relevance of issue?

JS, Channel 4: It depends on what the idea is.

CJ, PBS: We look for all of the above. *(See answer to question 20)*

22. Do technical issues in a trailer or work-in progress matter if they can be fixed later? E.g. professional mix, color correction, etc.

JS, Channel 4: No.

CJ, PBS: No.

23. What materials should accompany a trailer?

JS, Channel 4: A proposal on not more than 2 pages of A4.

CJ, PBS: The complete list of materials that must accompany any submission to PBS is available at www.pbs.org/producers. A work-in-progress, like all other submissions, must be accompanied by a release form available on the site.

24. Should a filmmaker spend time and money on a good presentation package or do these things not impress you?

JS, Channel 4: I hate flashy presentations.

CJ, PBS: It is solely up to the producer to determine what he/she wants to convey through their proposal. Demonstrating their experience and ability to create quality television are the most important elements we look for.

25. What is the most common mistake filmmakers make in their trailers?

JS, Channel 4: They think you will watch them all!

CJ, PBS: Not checking the dub before submitting it to ensure that the material was copied.

PART II
WARM UP THE ENGINE

Chapter 7
Topic-based and character-based documentary

You have your idea and are fully committed to it. But you are still not ready to run out the door and start shooting...not yet. There is more thinking to do, particularly if you want to save time and money while making a good trailer.

First, you have to figure out which of two very broad and vague categories you want your documentary to belong to. Will you be focusing on a topic or a character? This choice will become the backbone of your trailer and subsequent documentary; i.e., the story structure that will shape your ideas into a story.

You might think that there is no choice because every documentary has a topic. That is partially true, since all documentaries cover a theme. Your decision here is whether to stay focused on that topic or on a character. You can choose to explore an issue or theme through a specific character. Or you may determine that the particular characters are not important and the topic takes precedence.

Your documentary may even belong somewhere in the vast gray area between these two categories. Your job is to be clear about how your film relates to these categories. Exceptions make art, but confusion does not.

Character-based documentaries

Character-based documentaries follow or depict the life of one or a small number of people. If you are looking into an issue such as cancer or HIV and do so by following the struggles of one particular person then your film is primarily character-based. Biographies and personal documentaries are by their nature, character-based.

A narrator or host does not qualify as a character because they are not intrinsic to the story but circumstantial. Michael Moore's *Bowling for Columbine,* is a topic-based documentary rather than a character-based one, because the film does not tell the story of Moore; it is Moore telling us a story about gun control.

A character-based documentary can have one, two, or more characters. Is your character's experience unique? Or on the contrary, is diversity important? Does your issue allow for different outcomes that need to be developed? The answers to these questions can help you decide if your film requires more than one perspective.

In general, using more than four or five characters in the final film will dilute the strength of your documentary. It is hard for viewers to follow so many story lines. This does not mean you should limit yourself to following only three characters during the shoot, especially if there is a particular outcome you need to cover. Film as many people as you consider necessary. Once you get into the editing room, you can narrow down the number of characters you want to portray by deciding which represents the topic best. If you find that all the characters must be included, then you might be dealing with a topic-based documentary instead of a character-based one.

Examples of character-based documentary are 2003 Academy Award Nominee *The Collector of Bedford Street* by Alice Elliot and 2001 Grand Jury Award winner at Sundance Film Festival *Southern Comfort* by Kate Davis. *Spellbound* by Jeffrey Blitz is also a character-based documentary and probably one of the few with more than three characters, that we can follow without getting lost and confused. This is possibly because they are all pursuing one goal and are framed by the competition.

Topic-based documentaries

Topic-based documentaries have a theme or issue as their main focus. If you are exploring a topic like cancer or HIV and there is no particular person who carries the storyline, then you are making a topic-based documentary.

In a topic-based film different people can relate their stories, but they are not characters; rather they function as interviewees. The storyline does not depend on them; it depends on the exposure of different aspects of the topic. As with character-based films, you need to narrow down the many areas of the topic you will cover to prevent your documentary from being of encyclopedic proportions.

In *What is it about Hats? A documentary about the people under the brim,* filmmaker and milliner Andee Kinzy interviewed many American milliners and hat wearers. There are many ideas that can be explored within the larger subject:

hat history, hat etiquette, hats in other cultures; the list is endless. Fortunately, her film is not. She chose to stick to why people wear hats and how they feel in them. The challenge of topic-based films is to adhere to a concise narrative and to not attempt to cover everything about a broad issue—tell a story.

Only you can decide what aspects of a certain topic are relevant to your documentary. If you took the time to explore your motivation for making your film, this should not be difficult to determine. Once you narrow down what you will be covering, pulling it together will take some skill.

A hazardous but typical short cut is to use a narrator or voice-over as the common thread. Do not jump to this conclusion. Just because your film does not have "a" character does not mean it will not have character. There is a person in the film, you, and whenever there is a person, there is a point of view. Do not shy away from topic-based films; they can have a very original perspective and shed light on an issue with humor and style.

Another example of a topic-based documentary is *Capturing the Friedmans* by Andrew Jarecki which was nominated for the 2004 Academy Awards. One could argue that there is a character we follow in *Capturing the Friedmans*, but the unfolding of the event takes precedence. No character carries a storyline or shows an arc, making them interviewees of different degrees of involvement who contribute to the disclosure of the issue.

Topic-based or character-based—the consequences of your choice

Over the last few years documentaries have increased in popularity, both with audiences and within the marketplace. It is hard to tell what created this increase in interest. It is possible that the networks' need for audiences and more content pushed documentaries closer to the realm of fiction, making them popular. Or maybe documentaries were evolving on their own towards a structure mostly found in fiction and in doing so found a place in broader markets. This led to a preference for character-based films or films with a strong narrator.

In many ways the current demand for character-based films is quite logical; people relate to other people more than they relate to objects or topics—especially when we do not see the issue affect a human being directly. Have you ever noticed how at a museum people spend more time in front of portraits than they do in front of land-scapes? Characters transmit emotions that are more engaging to viewers than inanimate objects or bare descriptions. In films, characters usually present a conflict or challenge as part of the journey. This keeps us interested until we see its resolution.

But topic-based films have the potential to be just as engaging for different reasons. When the magnitude of an event surprises or shocks us, a topic makes up with intensity what it lacks in character emotions. The audience is pulled into the film not by identifying with a character, but by witnessing a powerful event. All documentaries on major disasters fall into this category.

If your topic-based film is not about a major tragedy, you will have to rely on other factors to make it appealing such as how you present the information, i.e. humor, style, visuals, uniqueness of the content, etc. You can also make your film appealing by being aware of and catering to the specific audience, such as hat wearers or Elvis fans. Sometimes a niche audience is more loyal and responsive than a broader anonymous one.

There are no wrong choices. Whatever you decide to do, you can use it to your advantage.

Chapter 8
What are the main story structures for trailers?

Now that you have an idea about whether your film will be character-based or topic-based, you can choose between two templates that you can apply to the structure of your trailer: The Structural/Dramatic Approach or the Free-flow/Descriptive Approach.

Both of these templates will give you an organizing principle to get started and will help you become familiar with your scenes in a structured way. Once your scenes are organized in this tentative structure you can continue to rearrange them until you feel the trailer represents your film. The important thing is to overcome that initial paralysis writers call the "blank page" and then feel free to keep searching for excellence.

Feel free to stretch these models or even combine them. As with all models, they should serve your needs and not the other way around. Do not think of them as a rigid glass vase into which you pour your film; instead, let them be balloons that will contain your film while allowing it to take whatever shape is required. Each time you add water to the balloon it will expand and mold into a unique shape.

Structural/Dramatic Approach

The Structural/Dramatic Approach is one template that will help you to organize the content of your trailer. It is more suitable for, but not limited to, character-based films. Topic-based documentaries that have a strict chronological order can also use the parameters of this template.

The main components of this model are:

    a. The Ws
    b. Key Event 1
    c. Key Event 2
    d. Cliffhanger

a. The Ws: Who, What, and Where

In the first minute of your trailer you need to convey clearly: WHO are the characters; WHAT is the situation; and WHERE this is taking place. (The WHERE is sometimes irrelevant, you need to clearly depict it only if it is central to your story.) You do not need a full scene for each W; often one shot or interview will establish all of these elements.

For example, let's imagine a documentary on women and cancer.

```
CU of an African-American woman, SALLY, in her
mid-fifties in a hospital gown.
Sally, "Cancer runs in my family. When the doctor
told me the result of the tests, it was no surprise
to me."
```

```
CU of a young white woman, MARY in her early
twenties.
Mary, "I couldn't believe it, I was speechless.
The first thing that crossed my mind was my two-
year-old daughter. I got scared."
```

These two short interviews clearly state WHO they are, hints WHAT the situation is and presents WHERE this is happening. We now know what type of film we will be watching. Establishing the Ws only takes a minute or two.

Since topic-based documentaries have no main character (WHO) driving the story, applying this model is not always your best bet. The Structural/Dramatic Approach works well for films with topics that function as characters and have a chronological sequence of events or a journey, such as with major disasters. A hurricane can be the WHO.

b. Key Event 1: Why

This is the second or third minute of your trailer. It will explain what action your characters take given their situation. It may even reveal your characters' motivation for choosing one action over another. As with The Ws, this also can be represented in one scene.

For our film about women with cancer, KE 1 could be Sally choosing to explore an experimental drug over long term and very invasive treatment because she was told she only has six months to live.

With a few simple scenes you have communicated what your characters will do regarding their dilemma and why they are making these choices.

Applying this model to a topic-based film is challenging and might require some maneuvering. For our hurricane documentary, the KE 1 scene could explain how hurricanes develop or cover why certain areas are more affected by hurricanes than others.

The KE 1 is what pulls us into the film. We already know the characters and now we know why we should care about them.

c. Key Event 2: Obstacle (random element)

Midway into your trailer, you need to introduce the challenge your character(s) will face and possibly overcome. This is Key Event 2 (KE 2), the obstacle or obstacles that your character(s) may encounter. This challenge should be of the same magnitude as your character(s), dilemma and raise the stakes.

In the case of our cancer documentary about Sally, the KE 2 could be a lack of government approval for the experimental drug or the drug being too expensive and not covered by her health insurance. Both of these obstacles are of equal measure with the situation portrayed.

One of the difficult things about the KE 2 is that it must really happen. It cannot be manufactured, just because your film needs a KE2 or you want a specific event. This is something you have no control over. That is why it is considered a random element. Even if you feel your film does not have a KE 2, look closely. Reality is quite complicated and might be preventing you from discovering the unique challenges your character(s) are facing. If you cannot find them the not yet written "Manual of the Ethical Documentarian" says you should not manipulate reality to obtain this element. If you are overly tempted to add your own set of obstacles to enhance the dramatic value of your story then consider doing fiction instead.

In the topic-based documentary about the hurricane, the KE 2 might be a scene depicting how the lack of resources prevents villagers from recovering and continuing with their lives. Because a major disaster and its consequences are the main focus of this topic-based documentary, it could be that no obstacle seems to be of equal importance. A series of small obstacles will do in this case.

The KE 2 raises the stakes of your story. While it is real, by singling it out you have identified something for your character(s) to overcome and given the audience a reason to see them through it.

d. Cliffhanger

Cliffhanger (CH) or Hook, or Terra Incognita as I prefer to call it, is a huge question mark looming at the end of your trailer. It is the result we look forward to finding out in the finished film. At the end of your trailer the CH piques the curiosity of the viewer and hints at what is coming in your future documentary. It is your way of saying, "Wanna see more? Then finance this film."

In the case of Sally, the cancer patient, the CH might be a scene in which she lobbies to get the drug approved. We know what is next, sort of. She is going to fight, but the question is, will she win? Will the drug be approved in time?

The hurricane trailer might have a satellite image showing another hurricane forming in the ocean nearby. We wonder, are the villagers ready this time? Will they get the help they need?

Sometimes rather than using a scene from your footage, the CH can be a slate that succinctly states what will happen. For example it can be an affirmative statement or a statistic that awakens us to the severity of the situation: 100 hundred women die of cancer every day. 50% of those die because of bureaucracy delays. (This is a made up statistic, but you should do your research and see if there is a fact that can enhance the overall theme of your trailer.)

The CH might change over time as you shoot more for your documentary. Your story probably has many potential outcomes to explore. It is up to you to recognize which ending carries the most dramatic impact.

Free-Flow/Descriptive Approach

The Free-Flow/Descriptive Approach is the other template you should consider for organizing the content of your trailer. Topic-based documentaries work well with this template. Character-based documentaries that do not have a clear journey, such as slice-of-life stories, can also benefit from this approach.

This model is called the "free-flow or descriptive" model because there is no inner dynamic that binds the scenes together. Rather than engaging the audience in the dramatic conflict of the characters, the scenes describe the situation from different perspectives. There is no specific timeline of action and reaction. The scenes do not demand a specific order. It is the filmmaker who arranges them to tell a story based on a common theme.

This template can be the more intuitive one, because unlike the character-based documentary with its clearly delineated journeys, in this one you must rely on your judgment and intuition to choose the best scenes. There is no "Who, What or Why" to guide your choices. Instead, your values and motivation will have to be fully developed in order to point you in the right direction.

The main components of this template are:

    a. Outstanding Scene
    b. Related Scene
    c. Review

a. Outstanding Scene: Strongest, loudest, most meaningful.

In the first minute or so of your trailer you want to present the highest point of interest of your documentary, the Outstanding Scene (OS). Out of the collage of situations that will form your final film, you must find the one or two scenes that embody the entire theme. You can recognize it because it is usually the one scene that plays over and over in your mind whenever you think about your film. The OS immediately lets the audience know exactly what they are getting into.

Let's imagine a topic-based documentary about bungee jumping. The most engaging aspect of bungee jumping is the free-fall, right? So you probably want to open the trailer with a subjective shot of a person falling through mid-air as the ground rushes up towards her while she is screaming in exhilaration.

Now, let's imagine a character-based documentary about two bike messengers. The characters are not fighting for better working conditions or a raise. It is just a normal day in the life of a bike messenger filled with surprises and small complications. Perhaps your OS would be an interview of one of the bike messengers saying, "Everyday I travel 150 miles, but go nowhere." Then you could cut to a shot of bike messengers swerving through rush-hour traffic.

The objective of the OS is to intrigue and excite your audience immediately, since you will not have the luxury of conflict resolution to pull your viewers into your story.

b. Related Scene: Adding insight

Two to four minutes into your trailer, after you have established a strong opening scene, comes the Related Scene (RS), which conveys additional information associated with the overall theme. The RS is either a scene that continues with the theme of the OS or is in direct opposition to it. Either way, you will be exposing one more layer of your story. It is also usually your second-favorite memory of your shoot.

In our topic-based film about bungee jumping, the RS might be a series of shots showing the jumpers putting on their equipment and sharing their fear and excitement before they take the plunge. In that case, the RS is related to the OS by similarity.

For the character-based bike messenger film, you might choose an RS that is a scene of opposition: Your bike messenger might be lying in bed with her bruised legs propped up on a pillow while she relates anecdotes about biking accidents.

With the RS you want to keep the interest level high. The possibilities for achieving this are endless. The most important thing is to keep the content flowing with new information as well as presenting visually engaging scenes.

c. Review: Exploring the Future

In the final minutes of your trailer, the Review (RV) scene will summarize your overall point of view for the documentary while bringing in further enticing information. The RV hints at the hidden aspects of the issue you are covering and should grab the curiosity of your audience. Be careful not to be too conclusive. Your trailer should not feel like a finished piece. As with the Cliffhanger, you want to leave the viewers wanting more.

In our bungee jumping documentary, the RV could be a series of interviews that reveal the most popular destinations in the world for jumping and the reasons for their reputation. These scenes zero in on your approach to the topic. They highlight what makes your film unique. It is also the hook. We want to know why people regardless of age, sex or race enjoy bungee jumping so much, which will only be revealed in the finished film.

With the bike messengers, your RV might be a slate with statistics of the side effects from so much biking, such as the high rate of accidents or traffic infractions or the number of knee surgeries messengers undergo. (This is a made up question; do your research.)

Whatever you choose for this section make sure it is in balance with your OS. You may have doubts after assembling a first cut. Maybe the last scene should be the opening one. Also keep in mind that the RV may change as you shoot.

With the Free-Flow/Descriptive Approach you should be even more flexible about scene order and choice than you would be with the Structural/Dramatic Approach. Flexibility will allow the right combination to emerge. And trial and error is the only way to make your best possible trailer.

Putting it all together

Remember the templates are just overall guidance to get started, a tool to make sense of the chaos of reality ahead of you and the chaos of dozens of tapes later on.

Once you have read through these templates you might think you are ready to grab a camera and start shooting, or that you are ready to begin your edit.

Getting involved with equipment before you fully explore these templates can be distracting. Instead of rushing into production, let these models sit in your head for a while. Let your imagination do its work away from buzzing equipment.

Your first attempt might not look as polished, but if you continue to fine tune your outline you will end up with a trailer that truly represents your vision.

Chapter 9
Need to swerve creative potholes to go on?

The mere thought of spending two, three or even seven years on a single film probably makes you cringe. But there are many things you do everyday for your entire life without ever thinking about them as life-long commitments. Nobody is intimidated by the thought of brushing their teeth every day for the rest of their lives. We think of it as brushing our teeth after every meal rather than something we will do until we die. Making a trailer is a bit more complex than brushing your teeth, but it requires the same steady, almost automatized commitment.

Keeping yourself motivated and working

Whether you are a seasoned pro juggling several projects or a novice with a 9 to 5 job, you want to use your creative energy wisely and efficiently. Above all, you want to avoid expensive wrong turns and dead-ends as much as possible to minimize the amount of heartache and frustration you experience while working on your project. The more frustration involved, the less likely you are to return to your workspace day after day. To ensure you can get started every day you need to create a long-term plan, an alternative plan, and a short-term plan. In addition, you need to provide yourself with the right environment to execute those plans. The more planning you do, the less time-consuming and frustrating the task at hand will seem. As usual balance is key, because while planning is essential, over-planning quickly mutates into procrastination.

Most of us would rather spend time plotting the creative end of our projects than thinking about the footwork required. Unfortunately there is a lot of administrative work to be done before and while you take care of the creative part of your trailer and film. As Morrie Warshawski, author of *Shaking the Money Tree*, says, "50 percent to 80 percent of filmmakers' time is spent fundraising and doing tasks that are not directly related to the actual making of the film."

Therefore it is very important when you create the plan of action that you include both the administrative as well as the creative tasks required to create your trailer. Believing that making a trailer and film is just shooting and editing sets you up for a lot of disappointment. If you measure your achievements by the amount of time you handle the essence of your trailer, you will find yourself working a lot, but feeling like you have not accomplished anything. You will also rush through very important stages to get to the part that feels like filmmaking, only to discover that those previous stages were essential to doing a good job.

So before you sit down to work out your mega plan, accept right now that *every-thing* that contributes to the making of your film is indeed filmmaking. Shooting is filmmaking, but so is putting stamps on your envelopes. Editing is filmmaking, but so is making dubs. By validating every act that furthers your trailer, you will experience a sense of accomplishment every day and create enough momentum to keep you coming back to your work. The goal is to keep connected and engaged.

The long-term plan includes all tasks, the amount of time required to complete them, and the exact dates by which you will complete them. This plan is more formally known as the production plan and is included in your fundraising proposal. But this is a version for yourself, with more details and personal notes, such as who can help you with each task and resources you can use at each stage.

Once you have listed all the tasks—the fun ones and the not-so-fun ones, the time required for each and resources—check with your producer or a fellow filmmaker to see if the time frame is realistic. Your enthusiasm to dive into the physical production of your trailer can lead you to draft a schedule that is based more on wishful thinking than on reality. We are all guilty of this, no matter how many films we make; we still believe we can make things faster and at our desired times.

When your long-term plan is finished and realistic, add a column next to it for alternatives. This is of vital importance. Having a back-up plan when things do not go as expected is the secret to avoiding anxiety, which in turn leads to fear and procrastination. The alternative plan is the answer to: What if…? What if the main character changes his mind? Do you have another person you want to work with and still remain true to your project? What if your chosen editor is not available? Do you have someone else in mind? Even the most obvious aspects of your plan B need to be written down. Do not leave your alternatives as mental notes; these tend to evaporate in moments of crisis. Suddenly, instead of being a well-prepared filmmaker making fast, confident decisions, you will become a high-strung filmmaker making desperate decisions.

Now that you, the well-prepared filmmaker, have a long-term plan with its corresponding alternative plan, break it down into manageable bits to formulate your short-term plan. What needs to be accomplished every month? What needs to happen every week? What needs to happen every day? Can you see yourself accomplishing those tasks day by day? If the answer is "no" you need to go back and adjust your long-term plan's timeline.

Next, with a highlighter, mark those tasks which you consider your forte and are your favorite. With another color, highlight those things that you do not feel you are particularly skilled at, but could do or do not mind doing. Lastly, use a third color to highlight those tasks which you know you cannot do or which you particularly dislike doing. Once you finish the coloring you can circle with a marker all the activities that are creative and leave unmarked those that are administrative. Voilá, there in front of you is a perfect x-ray of how your plan and you are compatible. This plan with its colors and circles is a map of how your creative process will have to unfold in order to make it efficient and joyful. But before we do further work with this map we need to take another step.

Using the inventory of your skills in Chapter 3, let's determine when those talents can be utilized to their greatest advantage. This next inventory will help you to determine the time and space of your peak performance, so you can efficiently travel the map you have just developed.

Inventory of creative time and space

a. In which part of the day are you most alert and creative? Are you a morning person or a night person? Are you more productive working on weekends in large chunks? Or in small bits and pieces during the week?

b. What do you need to do to get ready to work: Organize your desk? Grab a cup of coffee? Check your email? (Be careful not to let your preparation routine take over. If they become a tool of procrastination set a timer to cut these activities short).

c. What type of environment is conducive to your productivity? Café? Office? Quiet? Surrounded by people doing their own work?

d. For how long can you sustain your productivity without taking a break?

e. For how long can you sustain your productivity if you include breaks?

f. How long are your breaks?

g. What type of break do you need? A walk? Looking out the window? (Be careful not to let these activities drag you out of the zone of creativity completely. Learn to identify the difference between a break and a distraction).

h. What signs tell you it is time to call it a day? Breaks happen more frequently? You feel frustrated with tasks you normally enjoy?

With many aspects of your film, such as shooting and editing, you will not have a choice of time and space, but recognizing your patterns will help you to develop methods for increasing your productivity even within the pre-established structure of a shoot or an edit day.

If you are having a hard time figuring out your creative pattern from the questions above because this is the first creative endeavor ever in your life, you will have to work it out by trial and error. Keep a journal of your work hours. Note when you are very motivated and when you feel in a slump. Log every break and its length. After a few days it will be very clear what works and what does not.

Once you know your creative pattern, in a blank weekly calendar highlight the days and times that represent your peak performance with one color, the low performance with another and use a third color for those gaps of time that are neutral. Go back to the list of the activities that you both circled as creative and highlighted as your favorites or those you are most capable of doing. Transfer these to the high performance slots in the calendar. Now, plug the administrative tasks into the low performance area. Fill up the neutral time with those activities you are capable of doing but do not particularly like. In front of you is now a perfect map-calendar of how to maximize your time and skills so every minute counts and every task you do is meaningful.

It seem logical that nobody would chose her worst time and space to do the most fun and relevant part of her job, but we already know the tricks that fear plays on us to prevent us from creating our work. Furthermore, we do not make bad creative decisions with the best part of our brain. It is often by default or by accident that we end up using our worst time of the day for the most important task.

You wake up motivated and full of energy, look at the pile of paper on your desk and decide to organize all those grant applications, a task you have been postponing all week. You are done and feel great. Now you need a walk. When you come back you are already past the highest part of your creative curve. Unaware you sit down to write the synopsis of your film or an outline for the trailer and for some reason nothing happens. Your frustration builds up and you decide to move on to another administrative task. You tackle this quite easily but the synopsis is still unwritten. At the end of the day you accomplished quite a bit but the synopsis remains untouched and you wonder how this happened since you started the day so motivated. A written plan to remind you in that moment of euphoria to tackle the synopsis first, would have kept you evenly productive all day. Organizing your grant application can be done at any time, but writing the synopsis cannot.

Understanding your own creative pattern and respecting it is hard enough. Imagine how much harder it will be when you are working with others. Working with a partner, such as a co-producer, cameraperson or editor, makes it even more necessary to be aware of your own creative pattern as well your partners' patterns. We wrongly assume that all creative people are the same. They are simply creative and get along just fine. This is not so, and partnerships that work are more the exception than the norm.

When partnerships do not work, it is often not because of the disagreements, but because of the lack of understanding of each others' patterns. The incompatibility leaves no room to deal with the normal stresses of conjunct creative work. You might want to push on while your partner is already at the end of his creative curve. Or you might need short breaks often while your partner needs long periods of concentration to reach momentum.

This lack of awareness creates friction that is transferred to the project. You feel your partner does not understand your vision or is not cooperating with your plan. A power struggle starts apparently about the project, but what it is at work is a struggle to work within your or his comfort zone. Eventually the partnership ends or even worse, the project is abandoned.

To avoid this, invite your team to complete both the Inventory of Skills as well as the Inventory of Creative Time and Space. Compare notes and agree on strategies for working that gets the best out of both of you.

In addition to your partner and crew being on the same cycle of creativity, make sure your life partners, friends and/or roommates are also aware of it. Explain to them what you are planning to do for the next few months and especially how you are going to structure your days and weekends. Tell them you might have to sacrifice a few social events and to please not tempt you too much with them— if you know that is your weak point. See in what other ways they can help you concentrate on your creative work and still have their needs met. With a mutually agreed-upon plan you are more likely to succeed.

For the administrative work, you can adopt another strategy. Recruit your spouse or roommates to help you tackle the tasks that do not require high concentration. Children in particular love doing "grown-up" work. Socializing over these tasks is the dream of every workaholic and stressed-out filmmaker alike. This does not mean you should start a sweatshop in your basement. If your dear ones complain about your absence, sharing the work that can be shared may be a good compromise. Allow for real quality time afterwards. If they are happy, you will be more productive too.

Finally, do not forget to record your accomplishments no matter how small. You watched a documentary. Great. You came up with the name for the film. Fantastic. You bought stationery. Bravo. A task done is a task done. And many tasks done is a trailer finished.

Being in the moment

When you commit to a year of work, it is nothing more than committing to a single day of work every day for 365 days. Every day starts with the first minute of work. Every first minute is a microcosm of that first moment when you decided to begin the project, as discussed in Chapter 3. If you took that chapter to heart, you are prepared to bring that knowledge into the first minute of every day.

Spend a moment to identify what happens right before you sit down to work. What do you say to yourself to help you get started (or not to get started)? Is there any negative self-talk or a sense of boredom or a sense of urgency to take care of small tasks? Analyze that first moment and identify the breaking point that tips the balance towards going for it or procrastinating for the rest of the day.

Whatever you do, do not "maybe" your work. A salesperson once told me, "*Yes* helps me. *No* helps me. *Maybe* doesn't help me at all." If you say yes, go for it. If you say no, go for that and enjoy your free day. But the limbo of "maybe later" leaves you in that in-between land that only results in frustration.

Practice initiative in other areas of your life as preparation for the critical creative first minute. If you do not feel like cooking, open the fridge, look at the stove and pull out the take-out menus. Spend a moment standing still and observe your thinking process. Lots of thoughts will fight to be heard. "Ordering out is expensive and not healthy. But hey, I work hard, I deserve a little pampering and I'm tired. By the time the food arrives I will be fainting with hunger. But hey, no dishes to wash!"

Let your thoughts run wild for a moment, and let each thought have a chance once. No merry-go-round and replays. Eventually they will fade away and you will go back to the initial question and present it as a simple, initial comparative action: I can reach for the pan or I can reach for the phone; both are easy to do as a single action. If possible encourage yourself by remembering how you feel when you make good choices that improve your health. Hopefully you will go for the pan and the rest is easy. One action follows the other, and when you least expect it, a great healthy dish is on the table.

This overly dramatized situation happens in a few seconds and most of us are unaware of it most of the time. This process also applies to when you need to turn the TV on or off, mow the lawn, do the laundry, or walk the dog. Every task has that initial critical minute that you can learn to master. The first critical moment of creative work is no different, and the more you practice in your every day life, the easier it gets for those projects that are more relevant to you.

Whatever you decide must be followed with full commitment. Enjoy your take-out without regrets. There is no "should haves" or "must haves" to deal with. There is no looking back. You can own each decision as a fully informed choice. You exercised your power. At the end of the day, you might not have done your work but you are not powerless.

Another trick that works well among my clients is to make the start of any creative work purposefully bad. Take the power out of that first sentence or first tape of footage or first edited scene. If you do not feel like writing tell yourself, "I'm only turning the computer on to see if I can write the worst sentence ever written" or "I will write one sentence only, any sentence, and then do something else." You can shoot just anything or cut any scene, a silly scene. Once you see yourself in your workspace you are more likely to tap into that rhythm of work that generates more work.

By observing your behavior you can develop the rituals that are conducive to getting you started every day. What tricks work best? What self-talk is more effective? Is there a quote, talisman or photograph that acts as encouragement? Write down the steps of that ritual and keep it handy for when you are not tuned in to your creative process.

Once you conquer the first minute, you have to keep the flow going, which makes conquering all the other minutes of the day a little easier. To make this happen you need a quiet mind, a mind that cooperates with the creative process, a mind that is on your side. What does it take to quiet your mind when you are working? How can you fend off interruptions that agitate your mind and break your rhythm?

Learn to identify interruptions, what type of effect they have on you and how you can best manage them. There are two types of interruptions, external and internal. External interruptions are phone calls, people walking into your workspace to ask you questions, the computer acting up, etc. Earlier in this chapter, we discussed how to share your plan with your spouse and friends so they can cooperate. But even if you are surrounded by the most wonderful people in the world plus three nannies, interruptions will happen.

Can you determine what constitutes an interruption that needs immediate attention and one that does not? If your child is screaming at the top of her lungs, please go. If your dog wants to play fetch, hmmm, it can wait. Once you have been interrupted, how are you going to get back to your work afterwards? The first minute after the interruption is not as hard as the first minute of the day, but still needs to be conquered. Leave a "mark" where you were so you can slip back in. Jot down your thoughts before you stop to address the urgent matter that can't wait.

Save the work or write down the Timecode or do whatever needs to be done; do not let the interruption be magnified by subsequent disasters.

Hunger is another external distraction. Intellectual work and production work in the field burns a lot of energy. Keep food within arms' reach, especially for your crew. A hungry crew is a cranky crew. Besides, food carries the message that you care, adding to the overall positive feeling of the team. And remember, you are part of the crew too, so feed yourself.

Internal interruptions are all types of self-doubt. You stop working because suddenly you are not sure if you are a genius or a complete failure and the question must be answered before you go on. You stop because you need to check for typos or you need to find that other shot that you are not sure the cameraperson recorded. Doubts are all around; doubts about you, your material, and its quality. Doubts about now and doubts about everything you have done. Doubts are normal and necessary.

Listen to your doubt. It might carry important information about your work and how to improve it. Write down your doubts and keep working. You can always look at them later and discuss them with a friend if you need to, but you should not focus on them in the middle of your work hours. You may wonder in the middle of shooting or editing or writing, "Has this film been done before?" You might be tempted to either disregard the question or drop everything to do a thorough Internet search on the topic. No and no are the correct responses to both these reactions. Write it down. It is a valid question; you need to know what other work has been done about your topic, but you do not need to know at this very minute. That other film is not going to disappear while you finish your work, but your momentum will.

Not all doubts are created equal. Some are stronger and very valid and deserve immediate attention. Others cannot be addressed at all and are the fabrication of your fears. Practice listening to your doubts and categorizing them. Practice going back to your work after each doubt that has interrupted it.

Be also an example of going back to work for your partner and crew. Help them keep up their momentum. Are they deflated? Are they tired? Are they motivated? Be the vehicle of their creativity so your own creativity can flourish. Generous, nurturing filmmakers maximize their crews' creativity and the crews' salaries tend to be inversely proportional to the filmmakers personality. The easier and more fun somebody is to work for the more they will get for their money.

At the end of each day list your accomplishments and thank your co-producer and team for their own accomplishments. Each new day, review your previous day's achievements; they will help motivate you. If you got your work done yesterday, you can get it done today.

Chapter 10
Need a pat on the back to go on?

The concept that creative work can be accomplished by conquering the first minute or by knowing the difference between a break and a distraction may sound easy. However, if it were, we would all be doing it every day. All tasks are important and the trick is determining when and for how long to focus on them. Like anything else, being a productive creative person takes practice and knowledge.

Accomplished filmmakers need to get themselves to work as much as every beginner. They may have more awards on the shelf to help motivate them, or a full staff, but those things carry other doubts and distractions in themselves. The grass is not greener on the other side; they just get to mow it more often.

To encourage you to stick to a diet of continuous work, the following exercises will create memory cards of the discoveries you made in the last chapter.

Exercise 5 – The first minute of every day of work
If you took notes while reading the previous chapter you are ready to put into writing your strategy to tackle the first minute of every day. If you have not taken the time to do so yet, go back and re-read this section. Your creative life depends on it. *(See Worksheet 5 on page 81)*

Exercise 6 – Break this
Remember from the previous chapter that breaks and distractions are closely related. It takes some practice to recognize one or the other and deal with them appropriately. Rather than waiting until you are tempted by distractions, do some planning ahead by making an inventory. Or you can complete the chart as you work, so you have a log of your behavior and patterns. *(See Worksheet 6 on page 83)*

Exercise 7 – Doubts by the dozen
As you work, keep a record of your doubts. You will find that the same ones tend to return time after time, often in the same order. If you record their appearances you will in time get used to them and greet them with the familiarity of old relatives showing up unannounced. *(See Worksheet 7 on page 85)*

Worksheet for Exercise 5

My First Minute

In preparation for work I need to…

_____

_____

_____

_____

The seconds before I get to work I need to…

_____

_____

_____

_____

When I'm interrupted I will go back to work by…

_____

_____

_____

_____

Worksheet for Exercise 6

My Daily Breaks

When I need a break I will…	*For no more than…. minutes*

But these are distractions to avoid…	*By doing…*

Worksheet for Exercise 7

My Doubts

My most common doubts...	My answer to that doubt is...

These interviews are for you to get familiar with how people in the industry oper-ate. This information is not conclusive, nor exhaustive. When it is time for you to send out your fundraising trailer or work-in-progress, go to their website and look for the most up-to-date information regarding their guidelines for submission.

Chapter 11
Who are they in the grant world?

Here are two of the many grant-makers and foundations that offer grants to documentary filmmakers.

Independent Television Service–ITVS
Claire Aguilar
Director of Programming
www.itvs.org

For the past 12 years, the Independent Television Service (ITVS) has brought to local, national and international audiences high-quality, content-rich programs created by a diverse body of independent producers. ITVS programs take creative risks, explore complex issues, and express points of view seldom seen on com-mercial or public television. ITVS programming reflects voices and visions of underrepresented communities and addresses the needs of underserved audiences, particularly minorities and children.

Their team includes one director, two programming managers, one coordinator and one assistant in addition to the review panelists for the selection process.

Note: Feel free to cut out and bind this section.

Roy W. Dean Grant
Carole Lee Dean
President – in charge of submissions of documentaries and shorts
www.fromtheheartproductions.com

In 1992 Carole Dean created From the Heart Foundation, which is the not-for-profit organization that manages the Roy W. Dean grants. The aim of the foundation is to support filmmakers with grants that will enable them to create unique films which make a contribution to society and that otherwise might never be made.

Carole heads a team of 5 to 10 volunteers who devote their time to reviewing applications and deciding on the winners.

Chapter 12
What do they have to say about fundraising trailers?

1. How many documentary submissions do you receive per year and how many do you select or fund?

Claire Aguilar, ITVS: Approximately 1000 received annually; we fund between 15-20 documentaries.

Carole Dean, RWDG: We receive about 100 for each grant, the Los Angeles Film Grant, Los Angeles Video Grant, New York City Film and Video Grant, and the Writing and Editing Grants that take you to New Zealand. There is one winner of each grant. In the New York City Film and Video Grant the 4 finalists receive $500.00 each of Kodak film, so 5 are winners.

2. Do you select American issue documentaries or also international?

CA, ITVS: Both. Issues must serve our mission. It can cover an American issue or international. The applicant must be a U.S. citizen or legal resident.

CD, RWDG: We select and fund International and American documentaries, but our film grants are for goods and services, so you have to be, or travel to the city to which you apply in order to take full advantage of the donations. We take international applicants for the writing and editing grants which takes place in New Zealand.

3. Do you select or fund co-productions with foreign countries?

CA, ITVS: Yes, but the applicant must be a U.S. independent producer.

CD, RWDG: No.

4. What type of documentaries is your organization interested in: historical, social issues, personal journey, biographies, mockumentary?

CA, ITVS: All documentary (and fiction) genres are accepted, but they must serve our mission.

CD, RWDG: We have funded all of these types of documentaries. We want to support important films that bring little-known information to light or document outstanding historical events and we want to support films that tell exceptional stories. We don't limit our grants to any specific genre; we are interested in stories that touch the human heart.

5. Are there any styles you would be more interested in selecting or funding? E.g., verité, experimental, investigative report/exposé, etc.?

CA, ITVS: We are always looking for work that pushes the envelope, tells the story that has not been told before, that is innovative in style and challenging in content. Documentary, experimental, animation, docudrama (recreation), and mixed genres are accepted.

CD, RWDG: A good story, an important exposé, little-known historical films, and heart-felt stories that have lasting importance are what we love to support.

6. How important is the previous work of the filmmaker/producer?

CA, ITVS: Part of the criteria for evaluating projects is the degree to which the producer and his/her team will deliver the film on budget and on schedule. Clearly, more experienced producers are more likely to deliver on time and within the budget. Sample work is mandatory for all proposals, either finished completed work or works-in-progress for the project proposed.

CD, RWDG: We are very proud to say we have funded many first-time filmmakers and we have funded filmmakers with excellent prior films, so either works for us. It is the passion of the filmmaker that we feel is most important, sometimes even more so than experience.

7. What do you consider a good filmmaker/producer's track record? E.g., major festival awards, theatrical release, significant outreach.

CA, ITVS: We expect established producers to have had considerable success in distribution or broadcast, e.g., festival or theatrical distribution, exhibition at non-theatrical venues, previous broadcast on public or commercial or cable channels. We require that all applicants have experience producing in a primary role, e.g. as producer, co-producer, director or co-director—actively managing the creative as well as financial side of the project.

CD, RWDG: Important works of art that fulfilled the filmmaker's passion are what we look for. We do like to see filmmakers who are concerned with and plan to see that their film reaches the people it was created for and sometimes that is not the people who watch cable. We do like to see a strong outreach plan when the film merits it, both for their completed film and on the application for new films.

8. How important is it to have financing in place for you to consider the project?

CA, ITVS: For Open Call, we fund completion, either at the production stage or in post-production. There is no minimum fundraising required, but projects must be in production, not in development. For LInCS, the station/independent part-nership initiative, ITVS matches cash with the amount of money raised or in-kind, most often from a public station partner. The ceiling for the match is $75,000. We will often fund series at the completion stage, meaning that ITVS will provide the last monies in and that the series already has financing in place in order to be con-sidered for ITVS completion funds. We have limited funds for research and development funds for single shows and series, and there is no requirement on money raised for these projects.

CD, RWDG: Not important at all. We often are the first grant people win and our grant can help you get your trailer or demo tape made to enable you to get more funding. Our goal is to stay with you during the entire funding process with sup-port and guidance after you have won the grant; we want this to be the beginning of a long-term relationship.

9. What is the submission process? E.g., tape only, tape with press kit, pre-formatted proposal and tape but no other materials, etc.

CA, ITVS: We need a proposal and sample tape of the proposed project as well as previously completed work. For LInCS we need a sample of previously completed work, optional for the proposed project. Proposals are pre-formatted for Open Call and LInCS. Research and Development series and commissioning funding requires a proposal, biographies of key staff and budget.

CD, RWDG: We want a 2- to 8- page proposal and want you to include any prior works on DVD or VHS. If you have a demo tape for the submission, we need this too. Press kits are welcome and your budget and crew can be included but are not necessary.

10. What is the selection criteria and process? E.g., two rounds of panelists, unanimous vote, etc.

CA, ITVS: Programming staff review the proposals and make an approximately 50% cut, the competing proposals are forwarded to outside evaluators and readers. A 7-person peer panel reviews the top-tier proposals and recommends projects. Final approval of the projects comes from ITVS staff and the President. LInCS review follows a similar process and timeline. Research and development, commissioning and special initiatives are reviewed by programming staff and approved by the President.

CD, RWDG: Once the grant closes, our goal is to get the first round of finalist, chosen by 60 days. All who enter our grant get a free consultation on their application for ideas and guidance on how to improve it for the next grant. The 30 or so from the first cut go to the next round for a cut to 15 and the final cut down to 5 finalists.

11. How long does it take a filmmaker to receive an answer?

CA, ITVS: Open call takes between 5 and 6 months from application to contract. For others, it depends. Sometimes within a few weeks, sometimes a few months.

CD, RWDG: We normally have an answer in 5 months from the close of the grant, if not sooner.

12. What is the filmmakers obligation to your organization after they have been selected? Do you have input or final say during the making/editing? Share revenues of the film?

CA, ITVS: The producer has a production license agreement with ITVS, which contracts certain provisions and deliverables, including creative, editorial and financial control of the project for the producer; agreement that the producer adheres to approved program proposal as well as the budget, production schedule and delivery dates; that the production completes within one year of contract; that ITVS licenses the program for exclusive domestic public broadcasting and DBS rights; that ITVS retains a percentage of net revenues from ancillary distribution; that ITVS will offer the program to public television; and that ITVS provides packaging, scheduling, broadcast, outreach, promotion and website support for the program's broadcast. These are the basics terms of the contract, which can be negotiated as needed.

CD, RWDG: We have no input in the film at all. We ask that you give a rolling credit to all of our donors and that you give *From the Heart* the right to use your application for other filmmakers to learn how to create an award-winning application. If you are still using it we understand and can wait a year to put this on the site or to use it for teaching purposes. We also ask that you give *From the Heart* an associate producer credit.

If you can't use all of the donations, we ask you to let us give them to the second in line so our donors know they are donating to filmmakers and good films each year.

13. Would you consider selecting or funding a pitch or proposal without watching a trailer or work-in-progress?

CA, ITVS: In principle, yes, in reality, no. For Open Call, a work-in-progress or trailer or selects have become a mandatory part of the application.

CD, RWDG: Yes.

14. How long should a trailer be?

CA, ITVS: 5–10 minutes.

CD, RWDG: Long enough to tell the story.

15. Do you watch trailers in their entirety?

CA, ITVS: Yes. Panels often watch 5 minutes minimum of a trailer or work-in-progress.

CD, RWDG: We promise to watch 10 minutes but good ones we usually watch for more than that.

16. In how many minutes should a trailer "hook" you?

CA, ITVS: It should be interesting in the first couple of minutes.

CD, RWDG: Within the first two minutes we should be very interested in what we are seeing; however, we do have the patience to watch the entire piece to get the full picture.

17. Are the first two to three minutes of a trailer really critical in your decision process or do you evaluate the whole regardless of how the trailer is structured?

CA, ITVS: No, but a strong opening in the trailer is definitely an advantage.

CD, RWDG: I believe they are crucial to the funding process. I don't make the final decisions; however, I think you must grab our attention quickly, especially when we are watching dozens of demo tapes at the same time.

18. Do you think a trailer (5–12 minutes) is a fair way to judge a full-length documentary? Why?

CA, ITVS: It depends. If it's a promotional trailer without the feel, style or content of the documentary, then it's just a superficial look. If the trailer can contain these elements, then it should give the viewer a good "taste" of the project. Having a written proposal to supplement the trailer works.

CD, RWDG: Yes, because it will tell me how the filmmaker will edit the final cut and I can see their filmmaking abilities, see their photographic and lighting abilities, tell me if they understand audio and how good they are with people for their interviews. When they tell me a story with the demo tape and leave me wanting more, then they usually get in the finals. However, sometimes filmmakers forget they are storytellers and give you a history lesson!

19. In your opinion is a fundraising trailer more similar to a music video, a movie preview, a commercial spot or an excerpt of a film?

CA, ITVS: More like an excerpt, although some look like movie previews and they are more like a teaser that way.

CD, RWDG: A fundraising trailer is a story with heart and feelings and it needs to be compelling. It must make me take out my check book and want to be part of the production.

20. What should a trailer tell you about the filmmaker and/or topic?

CA, ITVS: This is a difficult question. It should give you an idea of the content, style, point of view and make you want to see more.

CD, RWDG: It should tell me that the filmmaker is fully committed to the film and that they are talented, passionate about the subject matter, and I need to believe they will complete the film.

21. How important is it in a trailer or work-in-progress to convey:

a. storytelling abilities?
b. filmmaker's unique voice or style?
c. access to the characters/interviewees?
d. relevance of issue?

CA, ITVS: : Important, but often difficult because unless you're watching scenes, it might be unclear about communicating narrative arc, characters, developments, etc. We want the trailer to express the filmmaker's style and voice. As per access, it can only be seen through the completed work. And we can easily see the relevance of the issue in the trailer, so yes, it's important too.

CD, RWDG: Most important. We must see that this person will do anything to get the right interview and the right person in the film. We also must see that they can get into the heart of the interviewee and get those jewels that make the film unique. The issue is important; however, it is really all in the passion of the filmmaker and when that shows on the screen, it can overcome anything.

22. Do technical issues in a trailer matter if they can be fixed later? E.g. professional mix, color correction, etc.

CA, ITVS: The trailer should have high technical quality, unless it's an Avid output rough-cut. If it's a fundraising trailer it should be of the highest quality.

CD, RWDG: No, but the filmmaker should state upfront, "This is a poor color copy," etc., so we know they know!

23. What materials should accompany a trailer?

CA, ITVS: Proposal, biography, budget, timeline.

CD, RWDG: An application with the reason the filmmaker is making the film. We want to know what will sustain them over the years it may take to complete the film. I like pictures on the application and a picture of the applicant. Also be sure to tell me the story visually in the application. That is a totally separate piece of art independent of the trailer and must stand alone.

24. Should a filmmaker spend time and money on a good presentation package or do these things not impress you?

CA, ITVS: Having a glossy notebook or pictures in the proposal don't really matter for us. It's important to be clear, concise and to express yourself well with written materials.

CD, RWDG: For us they always add something to the presentation. I look at all filmmakers as artists and I appreciate it when they put the proposals into special presentation folders or create them as a unique piece of art. It shows me that they too realize it is all one art form: the idea, the application, the trailer, the film.

25. What is the most common mistake filmmakers make in their trailers?

CA, ITVS: If it's a trailer, making it too long, i.e., 15–20 minutes. If the producer has that much footage, show it as an assembly of scenes or make clear that it's an excerpt.

CD, RWDG: The biggest problem I find is when I don't understand the story and when I can't find why the filmmaker is making this film. I don't see or feel any passion in the trailer and nothing touches my heart; it is then that I wonder how connected to the project the filmmaker really is.

PART III
ON THE ROAD SINGING HAPPILY

Chapter 13
Is it time to shoot and/or edit?

You have your idea, you have tested it and it works. You also have decided whether you are going to put more emphasis on the topic or the character. And finally you have figured out which story structure model fits your needs better. Yes! It looks like you are ready to pull out the heavy equipment, but not so fast…there are a few things you need to decide before you start shooting.

Many think that filmmaking starts with shooting. The truth, as you discovered in Parts I and II, is that brainwork is the most important part of filmmaking. Since you can ponder your story anywhere, you can start making your film right now. Do not let lack of equipment, money, and/or time deter you. Shooting happens in the eye and editing happens in the brain. With the right amount of forethought and planning, when you have the equipment everything will happen more quickly and easily than you expect.

Thirty years ago, the cost of film stock put a quota on what filmmakers would shoot—not more than 20 to 30 hours, which is a manageable amount during the edit. Nowadays, with the advent of digital video and inexpensive desktop editing, filmmakers have been thrown into Dionysian exuberance. Today's average documentary shoots 150 hours of footage and sometimes as much as 400. The ultimate paradox is that today's documentaries are not necessarily any better than those shot thirty years ago with 20 hours of footage. Needless to say, the methodologies for managing the edit and storytelling in general that worked thirty years ago will not work today. All the advantages of new technology have brought new challenges to filmmaking. When we try to apply the methodologies and strategies that worked for past generations to new circumstances, we run into pitfalls.

The Common Pitfalls

Some filmmakers argue that you have to shoot a lot or watch all your footage from beginning to end and let the material "talk" to you before you come up with a storyline…and to some degree this is true. A rigid outline with no flexibility can make you miss some great opportunities. But relying entirely on the outer world for story structure is equally dangerous. Documentary filmmaking is an exercise in Zen meditation. It is about being present and being alert. You are an observer of reality. It is your take on reality that makes your film unique.

If while in search of your storyline you find yourself researching, shooting or editing endlessly, beware. This can be a form of procrastination.

As discussed in Part I, it is OK and even advisable to shoot a little bit and maybe edit some scenes to get familiar with the equipment and the topic or character. Ten or fifteen hours is a reasonable amount of footage to help get the creative juices flowing, your technical skills perfected and get a trailer done.

On the other hand, when you are shooting or viewing your thirtieth hour and find you still do not know what angle you will take, one of three things is likely to happen: a. You will run out of money, b. You will become frustrated and anxious, or c. A miracle will happen and inspiration strikes.

a. You run out of money

Today's technology is affordable, and that is the biggest reason filmmakers run out of money. You might think, "Keep shooting, tape is cheap!" Yes, a tape is cheap, as cheap as $5, but you are not paying just $5. You also have to pay for someone to shoot the tape; that salary needs to be added into the cost of every hour of tape. Even if you are not paying a camera person, every hour of tape will add to the cost of your film once you begin editing. Each hour of tape will have to be transferred into a back-up format or digitized into your editing system. Add the cost of equipment rental and the salary of the person doing the transfer to the cost of your tape. On top of that, each tape will have to be sorted and the material organized either by you or somebody else. That is more time, if not money. Instead of digitizing material that will never end up in your film, you could be raising money and filling out grant applications. That single hour of tape will multiply its cost throughout the making of your film—if not in money, in very valuable time—yours. Knowing your storyline thoroughly helps you avoid this situation.

Of course, there are some types of documentaries that call for non-stop shooting, such as when working abroad in places you cannot access easily again, when shooting animals or natural phenomenon or when shooting events that will not repeat themselves. These are reasons to shoot more, but because you cannot control these situations, you have to be even more prepared beforehand.

b. You get frustrated

Without the right method for story development, 150 hours of footage can be overwhelming. Whether you run out of money or not, at some point you will get frustrated when your shooting or endless editing is not giving you what you expected. This emotional distress causes the shoot or your editing to become tense and not conducive to creativity. Some filmmakers turn this frustration and anxiety against themselves or even worse, against someone else: The shooter, the editor, the producer, sometimes even a personal partner. At this point the if-onlys typically hit: If only you had a producer that did her/his job. If only the shooter paid more attention. If only you had hired that other editor that was so fast. This is a dangerous moment where many filmmakers fire their crew, jump to another project or quit making films altogether. Do not blame your crew or yourself. Lack of planning your structure is probably at the root of this frustration. But there is something you can do about it. You can go back and plan.

c. Inspiration strikes

The other possibility that can happen is a "miracle," or what feels like a miracle—inspiration strikes. Either you get so desperate that you are forced into survival mode and finally commit to making decisions about your storyline, or the sheer boredom of doing the same thing over and over causes your creativity to kick in and saves the day. But the story does not just magically appear. It was there all along. You are just able to see it now. What has happened is not a divinely inspired event, but a side effect of spending so much time doing the same thing over and over again. When you engage in a repetitive, focused activity, such as reading or watching footage, the mind relaxes and begins to free-associate. A relaxed mind often lets ideas slip through more easily. This is called the right-brain approach, which works fine when you only have 30 hours of footage, but with 150...yes, you guessed it, structuring your story is the only way.

You might have a hard time recognizing these situations as pitfalls. So many filmmakers have worked through these problems and survived, that we all came to believe they come with the trade and cannot be avoided. For many filmmakers they are the stuff of legend rather than a trap to be avoided. There seems to be a secret competition on who has the worst war story, who has shot the most hours, or who spent the most months in the cutting room. More is not always better. Sometimes it is just more…in this case more pain.

Shooting: Finding the map first

Finally the time has come, and you are ready to hit the road—almost. You have a pretty good idea of where you are going and what kind of country you will be going through, but you do not have a map yet. You do not know to turn left at the second stoplight. Before you take the wheel, you need to create a map for your trailer. To do this you will need to visualize your trailer, to let it run in your head before it actually exists. Even if you have shot several hours of footage and are ready to begin editing, this exercise will benefit you and your film.

You have done your research and possibly even had a few phone conversations. You may even have shot for a few hours. So, by now you have a pretty good idea of your character's activities or the circumstances surrounding your topic. The next step is to sit back in a comfortable chair and start imagining the future. Yes, I mean exactly that—sit back and imagine, or visualize, all the situations that can possibly arise around your topic or character. Do not get caught up trying to foresee actual conversations or what will happen when you start shooting, because you cannot control these things. Just picture a variety of situations and take notes. A day later, try visualizing your film while you are doing something that does not require a lot of brain power such as riding the subway, driving on an open road or cleaning your house.

Going back to our example of the film about the cancer patient, what are the circumstances that you could envision she might go through? Will she have radiation or chemotherapy? Does she need to undergo more tests? What are those tests? Is she changing her diet? How does having cancer impact her personal relationships?

With these speculative notes in hand, look at the story structure model you decided on in Part II. Look at each element of your chosen model and find the situations in your notes that best match those elements. If you have a character-based film and are using the Structural/Dramatic Approach, pick the situations from your list of visualizations that best represent the Ws (Who, What, Where), the Key Event 1, the Key Event 2 and Cliffhanger. The same applies if you have settled on the Free-Flow/Descriptive Approach. Go through your list of possible situations and pick those that qualify as the Outstanding Scene, the Related Scene and the Review.

Go on testing your scenes and your model until you have a shoot list that includes at least two possible scenes for every element of your model. This shooting list will be your map during production.

Congratulations, you made it! Now you get to go out and shoot with confidence, knowing that everything you are shooting will have meaning within your story. If your budget allows for more than two scenes per element of the model, shoot more. Even the footage that does not end up in the final cut of your trailer will not be wasted, because it will be applicable to the final documentary.

For time sensitive issues such as one-time events, you will not have the option of limiting your shooting time. You will have to shoot the entire event for the full film. Brainstorming and creating a map ahead of time is even more important for these types of films. Since you cannot go back and pick up shots, you need to make the wisest production decisions possible in the heat of the moment. If you know the importance of each situation that you are shooting, then you can decide which scenes should take priority should you be forced to choose. Time-sensitive shoots are not the best places to stop and think about these ethereal matters. Batteries running out and chasing people down to get a release take precedence.

Whatever type of film you find yourself shooting, do not give in to the temptation of taking immediate action. It may feel more productive, but in the long run you will have to face your lack of clarity. Taking the time to properly prepare for your shoot will make you a more confident director and streamline your shoot.

Editing: The road behind, the road ahead

It's in the can! You have the footage—several tapes sitting there menacingly on the shelf. Or maybe you have more than that and they have been there for... ahem... forever, so you skipped ahead through these pages to get to this exact point in the book. If you did indeed skip all the steps to get here, go back and do them. You will still need to know how committed you are to your idea, if this film is topic- or character- based, and which story structure model applies to your film.

Once you know where you stand, you can focus on editing. Just as you spent some time visualizing before you started shooting, you need to take some time to visualize before you start editing. This time you will be remembering the past, rather than imagining the future.

Go back to your comfortable chair, but this time look back over your shoot. From all the footage that you shot, what jumps into your mind first? These are situations that made a stronger impression on you. They touched you in some particular way. And if they touched you, then they will in all likelihood touch your audience of grant-makers, network programmers and investors.

If you shot with a plan and did the pre-shoot visualization, you might think you can skip the exercise above and go straight to logging tapes. Even though this task appears necessary and productive, do not let it delay your creative work. Logging and transcription of interviews are certainly important parts of the editing process, but these tasks can easily overwhelm you. Or even worse, they delay the making of your trailer significantly if you have many tapes. You will in time cover those tasks when working on the documentary and there are ways to make them less all-consuming and expensive. For now you can trust your memory to select the most valuable situations for your trailer, which will save you a lot of time. After taking advantage of your brainpower, you can go to the tape and check to see if it is as you remembered.

Use the same method you did when you created your shooting list: take notes about the situations you recall and write down why you think they came to mind so quickly. Then place the model you are working with in front of you and see which situations match which part of the model. Go back and forth until you are happy with your list. The scenes on this editing list are the ones you will definitely need to log and digitize. And you will be happy to note that they will be fewer than what you shot.

You might find that you have several situations that could work well for each element. This is a good thing. There is no single way to do this. What you decide to keep or leave is what defines your voice as a filmmaker. This list will be a first assembly which will lead with successive edits to a more polished trailer. Remember, the models are starting points.

A crew of one or many

Flying solo or traveling as a group, both are fun and rewarding. The first is empowering; the second is great for bonding and can boost your own creativity. The wrong way to choose to work alone or with others is harboring false expectations about what one or the other really means. Working alone will not necessarily cost less because most people who work on films (crew members, camera operators, editors) arrive with a piece of equipment under their arm, which costs money. Working with others will not spare you from any heavy involvement, because let's face it, it is your film.

There is another key person to consider bringing onto your film, the one everybody dreams—the producer. Directors often fantasize about a producer who is a magical mixture of parent, CEO, therapist, and art dealer. Often filmmakers say, "If I could only dump all this administrative stuff onto a producer!" That type of comment is as likely to attract an enthusiastic producer as a personal ad looking for somebody to do your laundry is likely to attract the date of your dreams.

A good producer can be a great asset to any production, but like so many other things in the film world, it is a relationship. Finding this sort of business partner is easier early on. The partnership will be strongest if the idea for the film comes from both and is developed together. The most important element of this relationship is balance. If there is an imbalance of creativity or power, it will carry on throughout the making of the film and will be the seed of every argument or dispute.

A word about equipment

To buy or not to buy, that is the capitalist question. Is owning equipment the answer to creative freedom? No, but the illusion is so real that hardly anybody dares to ask.

If you have money pouring out of your pockets and you use hundred dollar bills to light big imported cigars, then by all means, buy everything. Get it all and have fun.

For the rest of us, the best we can do is use what we have wisely. I have yet to meet a filmmaker who is satisfied with the amount of money they raised for their project. "If only had I got that other $10,000 grant!" "I wish my uncle had given me what he promised!" The idea that with more money a better film could be made is debatable and impossible to prove. Rather than lamenting poverty, let's reconsider filmmakers spending habits: When to buy? What to buy? What are the implicit consequences of each choice?

There are certain truths that go along with every piece of equipment. No matter how hi-tech the equipment, someone has to operate it. That someone can be you, but you might want to consider first whether it is more convenient to buy the camera or pay a cameraperson that owns their equipment, or whether to buy the desktop editing software or hire an editor that is already set. With the price of electronics going down by the minute it seems pretty obvious that you will be better off buying the equipment and learning how to use it. After all, how difficult could it be?

It is not too difficult to learn the basics. It is experience that the manual does not include. Besides experience, you will need more than just the camera or editing software. You will need extra batteries, adapters, a professional microphone, headset, portable lights, some gels and a tripod. Suddenly, the inexpensive camera is costing you your life savings. The same is true of that inexpensive software. You will need more storage drives, a DV-player, maybe even an upgraded computer. The list goes on and the budget goes up.

My recommendation is that you start small, simple and with minimal risk. There will be time to grow. Getting too caught up in camera models and editing crash courses takes time away from moving forward with your film. Your main efforts should always go into fundraising. Before you head out for the big shopping spree, ask yourself the following questions:

    a. Is this your first and only film or you are positive this is going to be your career? Some people like buying their ski gear before their first lesson. It helps them to commit. I prefer to rent and see how it feels. Then after having tried it for a couple of months, I can make a decision as to whether I want to make a long-term investment. But, hey, worst case scenario: you can sell everything on eBay and recoup some of the money.

    b. Can you borrow a camera at least to shoot one day for the trailer? You can accomplish a lot once you get the trailer shot.

    c. Can you barter for services with a cameraperson? Some camera people are happy to shoot a day for a trailer if there is a promise of future work or if the project is interesting enough compared to their daily jobs. Many will consider bartering their services if you can help them out on another project. The same borrowing and bartering applies to editing systems and editors. Many editors work at companies that allow them to use editing suites on weekends. You never know what you can get when you start asking for it.

d. How do you get along with technology? Some people have a knack for electronics while others are still reading the manual for the VCR they bought in the 80s. Recognizing which type you are is key before you start shopping for the equipment. There is nothing worse than being stuck with expensive gear that you cannot even figure out how to turn on. Camera people and editors make their jobs appear seamless, but it takes a lot of hours with a camera to develop an eye for composition and an equal amount of time in front of a computer to develop an eye for rhythm. Of course you might be a natural or have a background that will help you make the transition. Perhaps you can learn the basics, assemble a simple cut and then ask an editor to work on it with you. You might have more luck getting an editor to commit to a piece that has already been trimmed down than starting from scratch with ten hours of tape. Explore all options and figure out which one is going to work best for you before you swipe that credit card.

If the questions above do not apply to you because you have a zero balance in the bank and cannot borrow a camera, think of the Rip-o-matic advertising agencies use. This does not mean you should rent Errol Morris' and Michael Moore's documentaries and re-cut them to make your own. Instead, think in terms of graphic material and sound you can assemble. If you are making a film about a historical figure, there may be plenty of archival footage you can use. If it is a topic like the hurricanes you can use news footage. (You can borrow the material from a TV station with a time code on the screen until you license it). If you have shot something but it is not enough material to fill a trailer, relying on graphic material can make up for the missing footage. Of course, some types of films lend themselves better than others to this low-budget shortcut, so think carefully before employing this method.

Chapter 14
You are done. Are you?

How exciting! Making a trailer for real, with real people, with real equipment, in the real world. It can be so exciting that you might never want to stop. But that is when you need to remember that the trailer is not the film, and the sooner you get it done, the sooner you will be working on the film.

Hopefully, you teamed up with an incredible crew that made your trailer better than you ever imagined. Or maybe you worked alone with the help of a coach or supervisor and were amazed by the clarity and depth of your own vision. With or without a crew, calling shooting quits is not easy.

Wrapping it up

Thanks to the fact that your trailer can have several incarnations before it reaches nirvana, you do not need to commit to a finished product right away. But that does not mean you should rush and send out a sloppy trailer. All those organizations you want to send your trailer to will be around the next quarter or semester with new deadlines.

While you are creating the best trailer you can make, be sure you do not give in to the temptation on the opposite end of the spectrum, treating your trailer as if it were the film. You do not need to waste time, energy, and resources putting together a screening for your trailer. Nor should you invite every person you know to give an opinion on the trailer. People mean well and they will all have an opinion. But opinions judge, and hardly ever evaluate. What you need now is a way to clearly see what else you need to do. To achieve that, once you have a first cut ask yourself these ten questions:

1) Is the main theme clearly conveyed in the first two to three minutes? If the answer is no, has the theme changed during the making of the trailer? Is the change for the better? You may need to restructure your trailer to accommodate the change or to get back on track.

2) Is it clear throughout the trailer who or what will carry this film? If the answer is no, you need to re-cut the trailer with this goal in mind.

3) Does each scene bring new, relevant, meaningful information to the trailer? Make a list of what information comes with each scene. Every minute should clearly add to the trailer.

4) Is there any scene you could do without? If the answer is yes, that scene needs to be re-cut or eliminated.

5) Is the footage interesting and visually engaging? If not, you need to go back to your tapes and do another pass in search of b-roll.

6) Is the sound (interviews and voiceover) repeating the information we get through images or is it adding to it? If the sound is not bringing new information, consider recording new sound, adding music, or remixing. Every element of your trailer should give the viewer new information.

7) Is the voiceover or narration necessary or excessive? Are there other ways you can say the same thing? Narration should be just one of your choices, not your first and only one for conveying information in a film format. You are working in a visual medium; the more you can *show*, the stronger your trailer will be.

8) Is the music enhancing the scenes or is it played through the entire piece? If you are using too much music, it is a sign that your scenes are not fusing together smoothly. You need to re-cut the trailer paying special attention to the transition from one scene to another.

9) Is the end strong and does it leave us wondering what will happen next? Your ending is your hook. Viewers remember clearest what they saw last. A weak ending can hurt an otherwise great trailer.

10) Does the overall style of the trailer represent both your storytelling abilities and how the film will be told? Sending out a trailer that does not accurately portray you and the film you want to make is like an actor sending out a headshot that does not look like them. It may get you a second look, but not from anybody who is looking for what you have to offer.

You can discuss the answers to your questions with your editor or coach/supervisor and fine-tune the trailer based on them.

As a fundraising tool, you should show your trailer to everybody, because someone will lead to someone who can do something for the film. Whether it is a money donation or in-kind donation, lend a service or find a new interviewee for the film. But you should only show the trailer widely when you are sure it is what you wanted it to be.

Before then, show it to a few select people in a test screening. As long as there is doubt, do not go around asking random people how to fix your work; that will only confuse you more. Keep working on your trailer until you have at least a mild sense of certainty.

Tips for test screening

The test screening is different in purpose from a fundraising screening and should never be a powwow of how to solve story-telling issues. During a test screening you want to find out if what you want to communicate is being communicated and that is all. You are not doing a screening to convince people that you are right or tell them how hard it was and beg for compassion.

Consider the following suggestions to get the most out of your test screening.

Who is invited?

It is tempting to think of the screening as a premiere, prepare a speech and have a ball. But this is not a screening to soothe your ego nor a celebration of completion, not just yet. You might have to go back to the cutting room and keep working. Therefore, do not invite everybody; save those souls for the real premiere of the film. Five people is more than enough. If possible, mix colleagues with lay audience. Or have separate screenings. You want to keep it intimate since you are looking to really listen to their reactions rather than to get a loud standing ovation. The less the better. In fact, you can have screenings one-on-one if it is practical and you have the time. Select people who are articulate and have a constructive way of communicating.

Where to screen?

Space speaks. It conditions the viewer, so choose wisely. You need a quiet comfortable place. If your cutting room or office is comfortable, fine. Do not squeeze people in a tiny hot cubicle; they will be more ready to leave as soon as the trailer is finished even if it is five minutes long. Conference rooms give the feeling of a focus group discussion. Screening rooms are far too big and might also lend an air of seriousness that invites over-intellectualized responses. A living room is more inviting and keeps a casual atmosphere. It sends the message that you are there to "chat" about your film and their spontaneous reactions are welcome.

Spare yourself

Since you will be vulnerable enough showing your trailer for the first time, do not take on the task of moderating the discussion. Five people might not seem to be a lot, but imagine all of them talking at the same time. If you feel particularly sensitive about the topic of the film, let a friend coordinate the gathering. Having a third party also helps to keep objectivity when the screening is over. You might feel everybody hated it, but your moderator can give you a more detached perspective.

First in writing

People individually can be nice, but as a group they have a mind of their own. Other dynamics come into place when people come together. Some people like to talk first, others like to talk a lot, others shut down when the discussion gets heated. Were you just promoting your film, a con-troversial screening is a good sign, but you are harvesting reactions and you want all five people's feedback. Hand out a very short questionnaire, two or three basic questions, which can help people organize their thoughts and commit to them. If there is someone who is overpowering the discussion, the more shy people are less likely to be influenced since they have committed their thoughts in writing. In the worst case scenario, if they do not speak at all you can read what they think later.

Listen and ask questions

Much as you would like to say your piece, share the litany of production disasters you had to endure and list the excuses by which your trailer is less than perfect, refrain. It is hard, but refrain. Let people talk and do not put anybody down. Even if it is the most inappropriate comment, smile, thank them for their comment and move on to the next person. Listen intently. People are saying more than just words. If you need to speak, ask questions. Especially if someone says something categorical, such as: "I didn't like it at all." Smile, yes, smile, or give a signal that you are not offended or bothered. Then ask, "Can you explain more?" or "What part didn't you like and why?" When they are gone you can practice throwing darts at their photos for having been cruel and inconsiderate, but as long as you are testing you want to keep a receptive attitude.

Record-keeping

In addition to the written questionnaire, you might want to record the discussion for later reviewing. Or you might want to take notes, though it is better to have someone else do this. If you are the one doing it while listening, three things happen. First, you cannot give your full attention to the person speaking; you might lose some comments. Second, instead of writing everything, you might unknowingly write only what strikes you as a valid comment at that moment, missing out on valuable information. Third, people unconsciously register your act of writing or not writing as an approval/disapproval of their comment. This is not something obvious but very subtle. Better to avoid it by having someone else take notes in the background, without being noticed by the guests and without discriminating good comments from bad ones.

Feed the lions

In the same way you fed your crew to keep their performance and enthusiasm high, you have to feed your guests. It shows appreciation and lowers the anxiety level in the room. People feel nurtured and grateful that you do not take their input and time for granted. One cookie speaks more than a million "Thank you for coming."

Evaluate

What to do with all those comments, questionnaires and memories? Compile, evaluate and take action. Compile the information by question and/or topic, such as comments on characters, comments on story, comments on style. Let it sit for a day and go back to it. With the help of your editor, go through and see which comments are justified and shared by others. By justified, I mean comments that bear some weight and relation to your piece. For example, someone might say that a character cannot be understood because of his or her heavy accent, and your character speaks perfectly clear English. Well, who knows why that person said that. Some people say things because you simply asked! So do not take every response as the gospel, choose the answers. Then highlight those comments that you decide to take action on and go back to the cutting room without delay.

This second round of re-editing is very exciting. Finally, you are close to the finish line. Do not become dependent on test screenings to lock the picture. You might want to consider other issues that deter you from finishing, such as personal ones or those inherent to the creative process. They are discussed in the next chapter.

Tips for submission

Now that you are absolutely sure this is it, you can go ahead and present your trailer to granter-makers, networks, and anybody else who will be receiving it in the best possible way. Your goal here is to make the screeners experience as pleasant and easy as possible, so that your trailer is never put in a pile of tapes that were rejected not because of their content, but because they were too much trouble to watch.

Cue it

Cue your trailer past the color bars and the safety black. Leave just a second of black; this gives people time to sit back, but not enough time to press fast forward on the remote. If they fast-forward your trailer, it is unlikely they will bother to rewind and your brilliant opening will be lost.

Standard Speed

You are sending out VHS tapes, which is the standard format as per the printing of this book. To make sure everything is OK with your tape check the speed and tracking in a couple of VCRs before sending it out.

Sound and Mix

Make sure your mix is mono. Yes, you will have to give up the stereo effect that makes your music sound so great for the benefit of being able to listen to your tape at all. Not all VCRs have a stereo function. Check your mix on a regular TV with TV speakers, especially if you worked in a professional editing suite. A mix that sounds phenomenal in the studio can end up sounding muffled or even worse, one of the track lines can overwrite another on a regular TV.

Label

Labels go EVERYWHERE. On the outside, both front and spine and inside, both front and spine. The label should be printed clearly and include the name of the film, the word trailer or demo next to or below it, the name of the producer, the name of the director, length of the trailer, and the date (this last one will help you when you have multiple trailers). If the trailer is in black and white this should be noted on the label; if not, format information such as NTSC Color is optional. Contact information is also very useful, in case your tape is separated from its supporting material. If you have a plastic clam-style case you can add a one-paragraph summary of your film inside.

Self-addressed stamped envelopes

Most grant-makers ask you to include a self-addressed envelope (SASE) if you want your trailer returned. Have your trailer returned! Make this a habit even when you are submitting to programmers and relatives. You might think that at $3 per VHS it is not worth the bother of an SASE, but when you most need it you will not have any copies of your trailer around. You will be surprised how fast your tapes will disappear and how difficult it is to find time to make new copies. And do not assume that by the time anybody sends you your trailer back you will be done with your film. Schedules are often wishful thinking. Even if you are done, you can recycle the tape; the planet will be grateful.

Types of envelopes

The bubble wrap variety is always your best choice. Funders usually will not play tapes that arrive in those fluffy envelopes that rain out confetti when you open them. The confetti can get inside the tape, ruining not only your tape, but also the viewer's VCR. It's no exaggeration! Play it safe; use bubble wrap.

Is this it? Yes, for now. Go over the checklist a minute before leaving your house to drop your tape in the mailbox and celebrate. You are done, at least with this part. You have accomplished an important milestone in the making of your film. But if you are not done, maybe the creative process is not flowing smoothly, causing further delays.

Chapter 15
Need to swerve creative potholes to finish?

You are almost done with your trailer or perhaps have even completed it, but now you are having second thoughts. Are you really done? Maybe you should go back into the cutting room or redo the credits. Finishing your project requires the same level of understanding about your creative process as starting your trailer in the first place did.

In the previous chapters, we discussed how to evaluate whether or not your work is ready. There is another aspect to bear in mind, and that is the internal sense of completion a filmmaker feels that allows her to let go.

In some ways, your project will never be completely done, because as a creative being you will always have something else to say, to add, to share. You may fear that you will come up with a better idea after you master the tape. And the problem is that yes, you will, but at some point you have to finish a project and move on. So, the real question is not when is the project done, but when are you done with your project, and how can you let go?

Artists have always struggled with this dilemma. Writer Jorge Luis Borges said that he published not to be read, but to stop correcting the manuscript. As you build your body of work, each project is just one stop along the way. A significant one, but nonetheless it is just one more stop in your creative life.

In the case of your trailer, this matter of completion is paramount. Your trailer is just a tool. Every minute spent delaying its completion is time you are not using to raise money or not working on your film. Hopefully, your transition from your trailer to your film will be a seamless one. But if funding is an issue, the completion of the trailer will be an abrupt stop until further notice and that stop merits your attention in order to make it a cause of celebration rather than one of frustration.

Completing the work within yourself

Your entire crew and family members are telling you your trailer is great, but you still feel that there is something missing. And you are right. There is something missing. You, yourself are not done. Your process is not complete.

This is the point when almost every filmmaker sighs, "I just don't know anymore." It is always the same words; the same defeated tone. It says, "It is done, but I want to hang on to it a little longer." There is wide palette of symptoms both emotional and work-related that emerge when the end nears.

The inability to let go manifests itself as suddenly changing plans, starting an entirely new cut, lying awake all night, becoming angry with your crew, returning to footage you discarded and any number of other stalling techniques. The unaware filmmaker may indulge in these reactions, and eventually settle down. They believe—sometimes wrongly—that looking for that one shot for three days paid off. But it is more likely that they found a way to dissipate their anxiety for a while until the next strike of creative despair, which may happen when the tape is already in the mail. Other filmmakers do not find any relief at all. They keep looking for that *something* that is missing until they run out of money or time. They let go by force and in a state of extreme frustration.

Neither of these scenarios are obligatory sequences of events. You can work on your fears rather than wearing out everybody around you. Those fears that haunted you when you were getting started were mostly dormant while work flowed. Sure, they woke up every now and then, but the concentration and routine required during the work quickly lulled them back to sleep. Now, you are about to be done. You are changing gears. Now, there is plenty of room for those same fears to wake up and come back loud and clear.

Fear of the unknown, fear of failure, and fear of success all need to be tackled once again. What are you going to do with your life now that you do not have the routine of the cutting room? What are you going to do with the trailer next? The questions generated by these fears are valid, and they should be addressed. But do not let them take over. Just as before, write down your questions and find answers that are supportive of continuing your work.

The most prominent fear is the fear of the creative vacuum ahead of you, which is a specific version of fear of the unknown. Once you finish your work you can expect a sudden sense of emptiness. This emptiness will manifest itself either as a surge of nervous energy or a complete depletion of energy. You may feel like running around the block and calling everybody you know or you may quietly curl up in bed.

Observe whatever behavior happens and let it be. If it extends beyond a day or two, start planning for a way out. When my friend Kalman Wagenheim finished his first book, he took up stamp collecting. Nothing can be further from Kalman's personality than stamp collecting, but the methodical organization of those little pieces of paper kept him focused and stilled the post-partum blues.

If you are a more active type, you will find yourself putting all your energy into showing your trailer compulsively. Promotion, fundraising, and marketing are all great. Be careful that you are not just seeking approval or looking for excuses to go back to the cutting room. So, stop. Go back to the previous chapter and look at the list of questions you answered to decide if your film was done. Also reread the answers from your survey. You are done! It is time to move on to the next step. Show and pitch, do not fish for compliments or solace for your creative anxiety. Not only does this behavior put you in a vulnerable position, it drives people away from you because most people do not know what to do with a filmmaker going through these ups-and-downs.

To avoid falling into either side of this abyss, plan ahead. What is your strategy to deal with the sudden creative vacuum? What works best for you? A hobby? A mini-vacation? More work? Watching TV? Cleaning your closet? Whatever it is, put it into practice. The completion of your trailer is a wonderful time to develop this habit, so keep notes on what works and what does not. These same strategies will be even more useful when you finish your film.

Progressive completion

Completion in filmmaking spreads throughout a series of stages. You are done to some degree when you have a first cut. Something structurally important is accomplished at that point, but of course you can change it later. You are marking an ending once again when you lock picture. When you add music, voiceover, or graphics, you are done again. You may submit the trailer as is, but later you receive additional funds and make a sound edit or proper mix. Here you are done again, even though you were done before. You get more funding and shoot some more, which leads to more editing. You are done again and again. You may even keep adding until, without realizing it, you have the beginning of your film.

Allow yourself to honor and celebrate each stage; get used to the idea of being done in small steps. The specific stage that marks a definite end for the trailer will not hit you as hard if you are celebrating all along. Help yourself achieve this state by revisiting your long-term plan and your essay on success. Are you there yet? How close are you?

Welcome your progressive ending instead of letting lack of money, time or other factors impose it on you. You may still have to say to yourself, "Stop!" with the same determination that you said to yourself, "Get started!" a few months ago. Sometimes working around your fears or understanding the process of progressive completion is not enough; you need sheer determination and discipline as if you were pulling out a thorn. It hurts when you pull it out. It still hurts when it is out, but after a while the pain goes away. Hopefully, you will not have to go cold turkey; it is the last resort and only applicable when everything else fails.

Extreme measures are needed because completion is not only necessary—it is mandatory. Being almost done can extend for months and linger until you lose momentum and abandon the project. Outside elements can cause more lingering-induced exhaustion. Your character might have second thoughts about being in the film. Funding might take longer than you expected. Reasons to quit are at the tips of your fingers every day.

Abandoning the project when you are almost finished with it may seem easier than dealing with anything and everything. But every incomplete project is an open wound. Creative energy leaks out of them. Even if you start something new, in the back of your mind you know that no matter how successful you are this time around, you did not finish that other project. Do not let this unfinished trailer be the cause of future fears. If it is past incomplete projects that are stopping you now, go back and address them.

Have you started something else in the past—whether a film or another venture—which you abandoned? What were the reasons? Are those reasons still valid? Make a grid listing all of your finished and unfinished projects in one column. Next to it list the status of each project. Then list the things that helped you finish the completed projects and the reasons for abandoning the others. In the next column write your thoughts. How do you feel about each piece of work? In the last column, write how you can make peace with your past work. What can you do to create a sense of completion? Can you re-use the ideas for future work? Can you acknowledge that their purpose was to generate new ideas and nothing else? Can you re-work your past projects into new shorter pieces?

Keep adding and working on this grid as your career moves forward. It will be a reminder of the interesting turns you have taken so that you could be here right now.

Go back to your present trailer and make a commitment to complete it. If you have not managed to complete many projects before this one, then use this as a way to break that pattern. If completion has never been a big problem in the past, then trust that this time will be no different. You control the fate and destiny of your trailer at this very instant.

Showing your trailer and dealing with rejection

Now you are done, really done. People are waiting. You send your trailer to all your wealthy relatives and apply to every grant. A small check arrives in the mail. You are happy. A rejection letter arrives in the mail. You are sad. Somebody writes to you saying they loved what they saw. You are happy. Someone at the fundraising event left early. You are sad.

If you are a seasoned filmmaker, you know this yo-yo routine, and the prospect of going through it yet again is not encouraging. In fact, it secretly fuels the fear of failure and might prevent you from finishing. If you are a beginner, your first rejection might leave you stone cold or your enthusiasm for the film may remain unshakeable, but your confidence in your filmmaking skills starts deteriorating.

Almost nobody make films to be rejected and criticized. The few filmmakers who do enjoy this mostly thrive on drama and conflict, not rejection. They love being at the center of polemic discussions. But most people do not enjoy this and are not prepared for the flood of mixed reactions a film inspires.

With a completed trailer you cannot avoid the problem of unfair criticism by showing it to only a few trustworthy people, as you did with your test screenings. On the contrary, your goal is to show it as many and as wide a variety of people as you possibly can. Instead of safe-keeping your trailer, what you need to do is keep yourself safe.

First and most importantly, you have to become fully aware that you are not your trailer, and the trailer is not you. According to Buddhist teachings, you are not what you have, you are not what you do; so by extension, you are not your trailer. It might feel like you are, after so many months of hard work, but you are not. The trailer is part of your work, but you are much more than your work. The trailer represents part of your skills and your voice, but it does not represent everything you are creatively capable of. This process of separating yourself from your work is called disidentification.

After you have accepted that you and your trailer are not interchangeable, it is useful to understand what happens in peoples' minds when they are commenting on a project. The first reaction is emotional, followed quickly by the need to justify the emotion intellectually. Advertisers know this. They sell you first on emotions and then follow up with all the technical information that makes you feel your decision is justified. The emotional part of the equation happens quickly. We determine if we like or dislike someone even before a handshake, in the first ten seconds of looking at each other, according to several experiments.

While these emotions may come through strongly, the justifications that back up these emotions are not always as clear. You will be puzzled at times to hear certain comments that seem to have more to do with the most recent movie of the week than your documentary. You will wonder at times if they watched the trailer at all. At other times, you might feel undeserving of the gushing compliments, and wonder if people are being sincere or just polite. Critiques, comments, feedback and opinions are all *interesting* to hear when they are not about your own film, but you have to learn to navigate them if you are to survive filmmaking.

To start, pay attention to your body and thoughts when you are about to hear a comment. Does your jaw clench? Do you hold your breath? Do you look down when you hear a positive comment? Do you always expect the worst? Or do you assume everybody loves your work, and if they don't they must not know what they are talking about?

Work on dissolving your physical reaction. You can take a breath or stretch, especially if you are at home and you have just read a rejection letter. Notice your stomach tightening. Stop reading and pay attention to your muscles. The idea is to break the ongoing association between getting a rejection and an unpleasant body response, so you can move through it more quickly.

The next step is to acknowledge your feelings, thoughts and fears to yourself. You are angry. It is unfair that they did not choose you. Your career is over. You will never make it. People cannot tell what is good or bad anymore. Go ahead, scream, curse, hit a pillow, write imaginary letters defending yourself, whatever lets the emotions out. Obviously, if you are receiving the negative comment or rejection in person, you should not vent your anger towards the person, tempting as it may be. Acknowledge your feelings silently. Move through whatever emotions emerge. Make sure you are not stuck in this stage for too long; set a deadline to leave the matter to rest.

Once you are done taking care of your own reaction, it is time to learn from the rejection and turn the situation to your advantage. As in the test screening protocol, always thank people for their comments and then ask questions. Or simply prompt them to explain themselves further. You may have misunderstood their point. If it is a grant-maker, call and see if somebody can give you more specific details. Be very polite; their time is limited and they receive hundreds of phone calls like yours. The feedback they are giving you is vital information, which can help you in the next round or with other grant-makers.

Feedback, negative or positive, will also help you define your future audience. You thought your film was perfect for Latino senior citizens, but everybody from Mexico over 50 who saw your film was indifferent at best. Well, it might mean that this not your audience after all. Women under 30 are reacting negatively, but passionately. Maybe you touched a nerve with that group. This is important information. With your trailer you can find out who your audience really is, saving you valuable time when finishing your film.

Treat all comments as an uncontrolled test screening. Listen, thank and ask questions, over and over. You do not need to take action on every comment. Not everybody is right or has a right to say what they are saying. Do not let them confuse you. Keep a steady course by always going back to your own purpose as a filmmaker. Why are you making this film? What do you want to achieve? Practicing being centered with a trailer will prepare you for the day when you have a finished film at a full house screening.

In the end, you want a quiet mind in the body of an enthusiastic filmmaker.

Chapter 16
Need a pat on the back to finish?

The day you dreamed of is around the corner. Yes, you are about to finish your trailer. The following exercises will help you cross the finish line and prepare for what comes next.

Exercise 8 – Strategies to deal with the creative vacuum
As discussed in the previous chapter, finishing a project creates a creative vacuum. Once you are in the vacuum, it is difficult to figure out how to get out of it. Filling out the chart below will create a map to use when you are lost in the vacuum. Create a list of simple and creative activities, like "read a book" or "go belly dancing" that are specifically designed to pull you out of that hole once you have completed your project. These are also excellent ways to congratulate yourself since most of your hobbies were left by the wayside during the making of your film. *(See Worksheet 8 on page 129)*

Exercise 9 – Role playing worst case scenario
Why wait until you hear the first negative comment to practice dealing with such feedback? Prepare yourself like an actor would, rehearse! In the martial arts, fighters repeat movements until they can successfully make the motion without thinking about it, and until their hands grow calluses. Develop your psychological callus.

On the chart below write down all those things you fear people will say to you in the first column. Include general types of people such as industry professionals you have never met and specific people such as your relatives and people you admire who might never see your film—from your mother to Michael Moore. Be thorough and do not hold anything back even if it sounds ridiculous.

You probably fear someone will say, "Hey, who would have thought an accountant like you would end up making a film?" Or, "Well, after you went almost bankrupt with your last film, I thought you would give up this filmmaking thing."

Maybe you fear colleagues will pick up on technical issues and think less of you. You could not get the camera you wanted and ended up mixing formats. Somebody notices, "It doesn't look all High Definition, right?" Or, "Is that all natural light, it's pretty dark, are you color correcting?" Ugh, and you just spent your last check on color correction. Write it all, do not judge.

In the next column, write what you think they mean. You think that the mention of your previous profession is saying you lack a film degree or the skills to make a film. When someone points out the mixed formats or the lack of light, you immediately think they mean you cannot keep the professional standard of your previous films. Interpret their questions letting your worst fears express themselves. Be mean, very mean.

In the third column, write what those comments could mean if those people you visualize criticizing you loved you dearly. It does not matter if the person is your sworn enemy. Just imagine they love you and wish you the very best. Mentioning that you were an accountant until yesterday means, "I admire that you could change careers, that takes courage!" Someone commenting on your many formats and need of color correction could be saying, "Hey, I was paying attention and noticed something regular people wouldn't. I'm a pro and nothing escapes me." Or "You did a good job dealing with a difficult challenge."

In the fourth column, write how you are going to respond to the comment using as a reference the third column, NOT the second column. Start by thanking the person or acknowledging their comment and asking a question that cannot only help you make a better assessment of their motivations, but also improve your work or yourself.

"Funny you mention I was an accountant, people seem to forget I am a newbie at this. I'm glad you brought it up. I didn't think I could make it. How about you? Are you in the arts or trying to pursue a passion of your own?" This approach opens the dialogue; you might win over a friend or even a donor—wink, wink.

So someone noticed what you hoped nobody would care about, your use of multiple formats that you are afraid makes your film look like a catalogue for cameras. "You have such a good eye, I'm amazed you noticed. Did it prevent you from following the story?" To your surprise the person might say, "Not at all." Your fear was unjustified. Now you are free to start worrying about something else.

After you have worked through your list, call a trusted friend and ask them to role-play the situations with you. Have your friend read to you the comments in the first column, one at a time. Get used to hearing your own fears and concerns verbalized by someone else. Scan your body for reactions. Then smile, acknowledge, and ask a question. Try not to frown or cross your arms or do anything that contradicts your words. Repeat the exercise until you feel you can deal with the comments in a relaxed way. *(See Worksheet 9 on page 131)*

Worksheet for Exercise 8

Creative Vacuum Plan

SOOTHING ACTIVITIES...	ENERGIZING ACTIVITIES...

Worksheet for Exercise 9

Dealing With Rejection Slips

I fear people will say...	They mean...(negative)	What they really mean is... (positive)	I will say...and then ask...

*These interviews are for you to get familiar with how people in the industry oper-
ate. This information is not conclusive, nor exhaustive. When it is time for you to
send out your fundraising trailer or work-in-progress, go to their website and look
for the most up-to-date information regarding their guidelines for submission.*

Chapter 17

Who are they in the festivals and markets world?

Hear are two of the many festivals and markets that offer a venue to documentaries, works-in-progress and fundraising trailers.

Toronto Documentary Forum
Hot Docs Canadian International Documentary Festival
Michaelle McLean
Director
www.hotdocs.org

The Toronto Documentary Forum is the flagship international market event of
Hot Docs. Launched in 2000, the TDF is the largest gathering in North America
of international documentary buyers and sellers in the social, cultural, and political documentary genres. Over 75 key international commissioning editors from
Europe, Australia, the USA and Canada participate in the TDF pitch forum and
each year over 50% of the projects pitched are successful in attracting additional
financing.

Note: Feel free to cut out and bind this section.

Independent Film Project – IFP/New York
Wendy Sax
Artistic Director
www.ifp.org

IFP/New York is a not-for-profit membership and advocacy organization, which for the past 26 years has been building bridges between creative talent and the film industry. The largest program of IFP/New York is the IFP Market and Film Conference, which provides an efficient forum for filmmakers to forge strategic collaborations long before they complete principal photography and enter the festival circuit and marketplace.

Chapter 18
What do they have to say about fundraising trailers?

1. How many documentary submissions do you receive per year and how many do you select?

Michaelle McLean, TDF/HD: Per press releases on website (http://www.hotdocs. ca/media_releases.cfm), approximately 120 eligible entries received for TDF's 36 pitch slots; approximately 250 requests for approximately 150 observer seats.

Wendy Sax, IFP/NY: 600-650 submitted, 85-90 selected.

2. Do you select American issue documentaries or also international?

MM, TDF/HD: The TDF is an international event open to documentary producers and commissioning editors from around the world. No quotas, but breakdown of projects pitched is usually approximately 50% from North America and 50% from the rest of the world.

WS, IFP/NY: The subject matter can be international, but it must be an American production.

3. Do you select co-productions with foreign countries?

MM, TDF/HD: See above.

WS, IFP/NY: Yes.

4. What type of documentaries is your organization interested in: historical, social issues, personal journey, biographies, mockumentary?

MM, TDF/HD: Focus is social, cultural, political doc genres in one-off or limited series formats with inclusion of natural science, current affairs, arts and history, and, as they may loosely fall within the focus and as the market shifts.

WS, IFP/NY: All.

5. Are there any styles you would be more interested in selecting? E.g., Verité, experimental, investigative report/expose, etc.?

MM, TDF/HD: See above.

WS, IFP/NY: No.

6. How important is the previous work of the filmmaker/producer?

MM, TDF/HD: The TDF selection committee generally focuses on marketability—so previous work will make a difference, but sometimes the subject alone can drive the package.

WS, IFP/NY: Somewhat, but not essential.

7. What do you consider a good filmmaker/producer's track record? E.g., major festival awards, theatrical release, significant outreach.

MM, TDF/HD: Previous films' record of sales and critical response.

WS, IFP/NY: Major festivals, awards, financing in place, prior distribution.

8. How important is it to have financing in place for you to consider the project?

MM, TDF/HD: Projects must have a broadcaster or distributor who has a financial stake in the project already to be eligible to apply for a pitch slot.

WS, IFP/NY: Somewhat, but not essential.

9. What is the submission process? E.g., tape only, tape with press kit, pre-formatted proposal and tape but no other materials, etc.

MM, TDF/HD: Entries cannot exceed 5 pages. See website: http://www.hotdocs.ca/tdf_entry.cfm

WS, IFP/NY: Online web application with contact info, key talent/crew, any financing in place, rights availability, summary, director's statement and mail 2 VHS tapes.

10. What is the selection criteria and process? E.g., two rounds of panelists, unanimous vote, etc.

MM, TDF/HD: An international selection committee of three chaired by the TDF Director.

WS, IFP/NY: Each committee member offers grades and comments.

11. How long does it take a filmmaker to receive an answer?

MM, TDF/HD: Deadline for entries is mid-February. Results are announced the third week of March.

WS, IFP/NY: Time from final submission deadline to acceptance/rejection letter is approximately 2 months.

12. What is the filmmakers obligation to your organization after they have been selected? Do you have input or final say during the making/editing? Share revenues of the film?

MM, TDF/HD: The TDF is a market so we do not have a stake in the production itself.

WS, IFP/NY: None.

13. Would you consider selecting a pitch or proposal without watching a trailer or work-in-progress?

MM, TDF/HD: TDF selection is based on the paper pitch but trailers are highly recommended for the pitch. Feedback from broadcast participants each year is to recommend that all pitchers present a short video clip during their pitch or have some footage to show them later.

WS, IFP/NY: No.

14. How long should a trailer be?

MM, TDF/HD: 1 to 2 minutes—must fit within the 7 minute allotted pitch time.

WS, IFP/NY: Up to 15 minutes.

15. Do you watch trailers in their entirety?

MM, TDF/HD: At the pitch itself everyone watches the entire trailer and pitch.

WS, IFP/NY: Yes.

16. In how many minutes should a trailer "hook" you?

MM, TDF/HD: Each one is different. In this case, it doesn't apply because the trailers are 2 minutes long.

WS, IFP/NY: It depends on the style of documentary. For example, verité requires more time than others.

17. Are the first two to three minutes of a trailer really critical in your decision process, or do you evaluate the whole regardless of how the trailer is structured?

MM, TDF/HD: Not applicable.

WS, IFP/NY: Both are important. Of course, like with any piece, you want the beginning to be captivating.

18. Do you think a trailer (5-12 minutes) is a fair way to judge a full-length documentary? Why?

MM, TDF/HD: A good trailer can tell the potential partners whether the subjects are charismatic, the filmmaker has a good rapport with the subject, and whether the filmmaker has an interesting cinematic style.

WS, IFP/NY: Yes. However, one should not downplay the significance of supporting materials (Director's statement, biography, production team, any financing in place?) and ultimately the final product.

19. In your opinion is a fundraising trailer more similar to a music video, a movie preview, a commercial spot or an excerpt of a film?

MM, TDF/HD: It depends. Unless a very strong visual style is a hallmark of the doc filmmaker and/or the visual style reference speaks to the subject matter of the film, you can do a disservice to the project and the filmmaker by making a trailer that reads like a music video. Having said that, there was a terrific 2 minute trailer this year at the TDF for an American doc essay hybrid starring pundit Lewis Lapham. It borrowed devices from dramatic film, music video and old instructional "How To's" to great effect; it promised style (fresh take on the essay), access to the subject (Lapham), and humor—something not generally associated with "the documentary." The style was well-suited to the subject—Lapham seen as a progressive, opinionated, etc. I believe the director had no director credits but lots of editing credits and field producing credits. Sales pending.

WS, IFP/NY: In our view, the perfect trailer should be a cross between a preview and an excerpt of the film as both methods have virtues.

20. What should a trailer tell you about the filmmaker and/or topic?

MM, TDF/HD: It should tell me that the filmmaker has a good rapport with the subject, and has an interesting cinematic style

WS, IFP/NY: A trailer should broadly present the main issues and themes, introduce us to relevant characters, invoke a sense of importance/relevancy/universality, and suggest the intended style. In turn, the inclusion of these aspects reveals much about the filmmaker.

21. How important is it in a trailer or work-in-progress to convey:

   a. storytelling abilities?
   b. filmmaker's unique voice or style?
   c. access to the characters/interviewees?
   d. relevance of issue?

MM, TDF/HD: It's all important.

WS, IFP/NY: The storytelling abilities are important but the style must support that. The filmmaker's voice is also very important and the director's statement helps round it out. For the access to the characters, yes, it's important and the supporting materials can supplement that. The relevance of the issue is important but not to the detriment of the above.

22. Do technical issues in a trailer matter if they can be fixed later? E.g., professional mix, color correction, etc.

MM, TDF/HD: Yes, because they are the first impression. It really depends on whether the filmmaker can provide a context and introduction or whether the tape is seen "cold" by the buyer. If the trailer is being shown in a private meeting with the buyer and the filmmaker can talk them through it, it's a very different thing. If the material was shot under extreme conditions—dangerous or rare—that might also excuse bad sound or image, too.

WS, IFP/NY: No.

23. What materials should accompany a trailer?

MM, TDF/HD: At the TDF they are accompanied by the live pitch, i.e., quite a bit of context.

WS, IFP/NY: For the IFP Market, a completed application form with contact info, key talent/crew, any financing in place, rights availability, summary, directors statement and mail 2 VHS tapes.

24. Should a filmmaker spend time and money on a good presentation package or do these things not impress you?

MM, TDF/HD: Not applicable.

WS, IFP/NY: No, not necessary.

25. What is the most common mistake filmmakers make in their trailers?

MM, TDF/HD: Not understanding that they require craft and style, too, and simultaneously that they must be true to the final film.

WS, IFP/NY: Not having a well-defined idea.

CONCLUSION

CONCLUSION

A t the end of each book there is a new beginning for the reader. It is a chance to reconsider the words written, to take action on them, to rearrange the knowledge or to even forget what was read and maybe to remember it again.

I truly hope at this point that this book is disintegrating in your hands. Pages are cut out and adorning your desk. Margins are filled with your notes. Entire paragraphs are highlighted in different colors. Index cards are inserted at intervals with random thoughts. Flags and post-its are waving from the edges like carnival garlands celebrating your creativity and determination.

If this book was deconstructed and engulfed by your vision and the voice of your future film, you can rest assured that a great documentary is awaiting you, as yet un-made, but eager to be realized. If the book is intact, the process is still in place and its results will emerge in time.

You learned in the previous chapters how to create the message, navigate the personal labyrinth of creativity and get closer to the audience you are going to address, so you can be prepared to have a more complete experience with your next documentary.

As reality keeps unfolding in front of you, enter it with your critical eye behind the viewfinder, a compassionate ear for your interviewees and a gentle hand on the record button.

Dare to succeed on your own terms.

Fernanda Rossi

A fiscal sponsor is a non-profit organization (501(c)(3) status) which allows you to receive deductible donations from individuals and foundations. Tax deductions are an incentive for those considering making a contribution to your project. Some grant foundations only award funding to non-profit organizations or individuals who have a fiscal sponsor.

The organizations offering fiscal sponsorship usually require a membership fee and/or an application fee. In addition, they may or may not be, a media organization, but if they are, you can benefit from their other programs and events by becoming a member.

Fiscal sponsors in general take a percentage (3%–10%) of the contributions you receive in order to administer your account. They are legally responsible for the funds you receive through them and must insure that the contributions are used for the purposes you stipulated. This is why grant foundations demand in some cases that you have a fiscal sponsor; it reassures them that someone is watching what is being done with their funds.

Below you can find some of the fiscal sponsor organizations around the country that are also involved in media. The logistics of how to apply, percentage they take, frequency with which they forward the funds to you, and all other requirements vary from organization to organization. Start your research early; the application submissions are sometimes only quarterly and you will need to present several materials. Their websites have all the information you need. Visit and spend enough time finding the information before you call them with questions.

Only you can make the decision of what organization is best for you and your film. However, if you are a first-time filmmaker, I would recommend you join a media organization in your area so you can meet the film community in your city as well as take advantage of their workshops, programs and events.

Center for Independent Documentary
680 South Main St.
Sharon, MA 02067
781/784-3627
781/784-8254 fax
info@documentaries.org
www.documentaries.org

Downtown Community Television Center (DCTV)
87 Lafayette Street
New York, NY 10013
212/966-4510
212/219-0248 fax
tish@dctvny.org
www.dctvny.org

Film Arts Foundation
145 Ninth Street, #101
San Francisco, CA 94103
415/552-8760
415/552-0882 fax
info@filmarts.org
www.filmarts.org

Film/Video Arts (FVA)
462 Broadway, Ste. 520
New York, NY 10013
212/941-8787
212/219-8924 fax
dcbutler@fva.com
www.fva.com

International Documentary Association
1201 West 5th St., Ste. M320
Los Angeles, CA 90017
213/534-3600
213/534-3610 fax
info@documentary.org
www.documentary.org

New York Foundation for the Arts (NYFA)
155 Avenue of the Americas, 14th Fl.
New York, NY 10013
212/366-6900
212/366-1778 fax
nyfainfo@nyfa.org
www.nyfa.org

Independent Pictures sponsor of
Ohio Independent Film Festival
1392 West 65th Street
Cleveland, OH 44102
216/651-7315
216/651-7317 fax
OhioIndieFilmFest@juno.com
www.ohiofilms.com

Public Media, Inc.
330 West 42nd St
32nd Floor
New York NY 10036
publicmediainc@aol.com
www.PublicMediaInc.org

Third World Newsreel Production Workshop
545 Eighth Avenue, 10th Floor
New York, NY 10018
212/947-9277
212/594-6417 fax
twn@twn.org
www.twn.org

Women Make Movies
462 Broadway, Ste. 500WS
New York, NY 10013
212/925-0606
212/925-2052 fax
info@wmm.com
www.wmm.com